Successful Job Search Strategies for the Disabled:

Understanding the ADA

OTHER BOOKS BY JEFFREY G. ALLEN

How to Turn an Interview into a Job
(also available on audiocassette)

Finding the Right Job at Midlife

The Placement Strategy Handbook

The Employee Termination Handbook

Placement Management

Surviving Corporate Downsizing

The Complete Q&A Job Interview Book

The Perfect Job Reference

The National Placement Law Center Fee Collection Guide

The Perfect Follow-Up Method to Get the Job

Jeff Allen's Best: The Resume

Jeff Allen's Best: Get the Interview

Jeff Allen's Best: Win the Job

Complying with the ADA: A Small Business Guide to Hiring and Employing the Disabled

Successful Job Search Strategies for the Disabled

Understanding the ADA

Jeffrey G. Allen, J.D., C.P.C.

John Wiley & Sons, Inc.
New York • Chichester • Brisbane • Toronto • Singapore

This publication is designed to provide accurate and authoritative
information in regard to the subject matter covered. It is sold with the
understanding that the publisher is not engaged in rendering legal,
accounting, or other professional services. If legal advice or other
expert assistance is required, the services of a competent professional
person should be sought. From a *Declaration of Principles jointly
adopted by a Committee of the American Bar Association and a
Committee of Publishers.*

Library of Congress Cataloging-in-Publication Data:

Allen, Jeffrey G.
    Successful job search strategies for the disabled : understanding
the ADA / by Jeffrey G. Allen.
        p.   cm.
    Includes bibliographical references.
    ISBN 0-471-59234-X (cloth : alk. paper).—ISBN 0-471-59235-8
(pbk. : alk. paper)
    1. Vocational guidance for the handicapped—United States.   2. Job
hunting—United States.   3. Handicapped—Employment—Law and
legislation—United States.   I. Title.
HV1568.5.A48   1994
650.14′087—dc20   93-23848

Printed in the United States of America

10   9   8   7   6   5   4   3   2   1

Dedicated to changing the phrase *reasonable accommodation* to *real acceptance.*

With appreciation ...

To my wife, Bev;
to our daughter, Angela;
to an editor's editor, Mike Hamilton;
to his assistant, Elena Paperny; and
to Pat Stahl,
    the most capable researcher any author could want.

Thanks more than words can say.

About the Author

Jeffrey G. Allen, J.D., C.P.C., is America's foremost employment attorney. For almost a decade, Mr. Allen was a human resources manager with small business employers or small divisions of major companies. This direct experience has been coupled with his employment law practice over the past 18 years. As a certified placement counselor, certified employment specialist, and professional negotiator, Mr. Allen is highly qualified to write this guidebook for jobseekers with disabilities.

Mr. Allen is the author of more best-selling books in the employment field than anyone else. Among them are *How to Turn an Interview into a Job, Finding the Right Job at Midlife, The Employee Termination Handbook, The Placement Strategy Handbook, Placement Management, The Complete Q&A Job Interview Book, The Perfect Job Reference, The Perfect Follow-Up Method to Get the Job*, the popular three-book series *Jeff Allen's Best* and, most recently, *Complying with the ADA*. He writes a nationally syndicated column entitled "Placements and The Law," conducts seminars, and is regularly featured in television, radio, and newspaper interviews.

Mr. Allen has served as director of the National Placement Law Center, Special Advisor to the American Employment Association, General Counsel to the California Association of Personnel Consultants, judge pro tem, and is recognized as the nation's foremost employment attorney.

Contents

Introduction

Today jobseekers have a lot of available resources—resume-writing services, career counselors, placement offices, employment agencies, executive recruiters, self-assessment programs, you name it. But in my experience, the jobseeker's most precious resource comes from within. It is a question of attitude. Landing a job involves salesmanship and a certain amount of showmanship, yet many of us are uncomfortable with these roles—especially when the commodity is ourselves. But if you don't believe in yourself and you don't project an image of self-confidence, you'll never convince an employer to offer you a job.

Maybe you can't move mountains. But you might be able to build bridges, program computers, or do research. Considering that FDR ran the country from a wheelchair, you should be quite optimistic.

It's not easy to develop a positive self-image when you face discrimination in so many areas of life, but remember that you are not alone. There are some 43 million Americans with disabilities. Consider these statistics from the National Center for Medical Rehabilitation Research:

- People with hearing impairments: 22 million, including 2 million who are deaf.
- People who are totally blind: 120,000.
- People who are legally blind: 60,000.
- People with epilepsy: 2 million.
- People who use wheelchairs: 1 million.
- People who are partially or completely paralyzed: 1.2 million.
- People with speech impairments: 2.1 million.

- People with developmental disabilities such as cerebral palsy: 9.2 million.
- People with mental retardation: between 2 and 2.5 million. Nine out of 10 cases are mild retardation.
- People with mental illness: 5 million, according to the National Institute on Mental Health.

Despite their numbers, people with disabilities are considered a minority group in this country. But they are a unique minority, with members from every race and religion, both sexes, and all ages. And membership in this group can be conferred on anyone at any time. It doesn't take much: a fall, a car accident, a slip in the bathtub, or a wrong dose of medicine. In fact, only about one in every six people with disabilities was born disabled. Many refer to a person who is not disabled as TAB, or temporarily able-bodied.[1]

Although their unemployment rate is currently more than 60 percent, people with disabilities actively participated in the labor force for a brief period. During World War II, when most working-age men were fighting, employers had to hire people they would not otherwise have considered, including women and people with disabilities. More than 80 percent of the nation's industries added disabled workers. The Ford Motor Company alone hired 11,000. And these workers proved their worth. Businesses reported lower turnover, less absenteeism, fewer accidents, and production rates that equaled or exceeded previous norms.

But when the veterans returned, workers with disabilities—despite their solid performance—were pushed out of the job market, and it has been a long road back.

History shows that public attitudes toward minorities—African Americans, women, gays—move along a continuum, from fear and hostility to acceptance. We have come a long way, but we still haven't reached the end of the continuum with regard to people with disabilities.

Case in point: A 1991 Harris survey asked more than 1,200 people nationwide how they felt in encounters with people with severe disabilities. Although an overwhelming majority (92 percent) felt admiration, it is tinged with other, more problematic reactions. About 75 percent of them felt pity; nearly 60 percent felt awkward and embarrassed because they didn't know how to act or what sort of help to offer; and nearly half felt afraid or guilty in the presence of a disabled person. The survey concluded that "anything that could be done to alleviate current feelings of awkwardness would go

---

[1]Sonny Kleinfield, *The Hidden Minority: America's Handicapped* (Boston: Little, Brown, 1977), 23.

a long way toward removing a significant obstacle to increased participation."[2]

The experts all agree that the only real way to change attitudes is through contact, and that's what the Americans with Disabilities Act (ADA) is all about. As people with disabilities participate more fully in the mainstream of life, they will be accepted on an equal footing.

The workplace is a critical arena for change, and attitudes here appear to be improving. More than 900 managers who participated in a 1987 Harris Poll had this to say about people with disabilities who worked for them:

• Eighty-eight percent of top managers gave employees with disabilities an "excellent" (24 percent) or "good" (64 percent) rating on job performance. They said employees with disabilities work as hard or harder than those who do not have a disability.
• Thirty-nine percent of line managers rated employees with disabilities as better on attendance and punctuality than nondisabled employees, and 40 percent rated them about the same.
• Seventy-five percent of the employers surveyed indicated that the average cost of hiring people with disabilities was the same as hiring a person without a disability.

Despite their positive experiences, most managers in the survey gave recruitment of disabled people a very low priority and noted very little pressure on them to improve their efforts. Only 43 percent of the equal employment opportunity (EEO) officers surveyed said that their companies had hired people with disabilities.

The legislation is in place. The important thing now is to see that it is translated into action. You can start by taking charge of your career and setting out to land a job that's equal to your talents. Yes, there is a risk of rejection, but the real risk is in doing nothing.

Doing nothing is the biggest handicap of all. Here's how to get going. Good luck.

---

[2]*Public Attitudes Toward People with Disabilities.* A survey conducted by Louis Harris for the National Organization on Disability, 1991.

CHAPTER ONE

Overview
of the ADA

On July 20, 1990, President Bush fulfilled a campaign promise by signing into law the Americans with Disabilities Act (ADA), regarded by many as the most sweeping piece of legislation since the Civil Rights Act of 1964. The new law will require changes in the way businesses and public facilities operate. Some of these changes will be physical and will cost money; others will involve adopting new attitudes toward people with disabilities.

The ADA is essentially an amalgam of two major civil rights statutes: the Civil Rights Act of 1964 and the Rehabilitation Act of 1973. The ADA uses the framework of Titles II and VII of the Civil Rights Act of 1964 to provide coverage and enforcement and the framework of the Rehabilitation Act of 1973 to define disability and to determine what constitutes discrimination.

But whereas the Rehabilitation Act prohibited only those doing business with the federal government or receiving federal financial assistance from discriminating against qualified *individuals with handicaps* (the term used under that law), the ADA reaches into the private sector as well, affecting both large and small businesses.

The ADA does not merely prohibit discrimination as does Title VII of the Civil Rights Act. It imposes additional affirmative obligations upon businesses to accommodate the needs of people with disabilities and to promote their economic independence.

In addition to the federal laws, more than 40 states have their own laws protecting individuals with disabilities. The scope of protection under these laws varies greatly. In congressional hearings on the ADA, former attorney general Richard Thornburgh argued that this new law weaves together the torn patchwork of existing federal and state legislation regarding people with disabilities and closes gaps in coverage.

RECAP OF TITLES I THROUGH V

The ADA prohibits both intentional and unintentional discrimination in five broad areas. Title I specifically addresses employment issues, but the other provisions in the ADA all touch upon your ability to find employment. A full implementation schedule is shown in Figure 1.1.

Title I: Employment. Title VII of the Civil Rights Act of 1964 opened the doors of American business to minorities and women. Title I of the ADA offers the same promise to qualified individuals with disabilities. It requires employers to take immediate action to provide "reasonable accommodations" to both employees and job applicants for a broad range of mental and physical disabilities. We will take a closer look at Title I provisions in the next few pages.

Title II: State and local governments and public services. This title prohibits public entities from discriminating against qualified individuals with disabilities or excluding them from participating in their services, programs, or activities. The ADA's guarantee of full participation in the mainstream of American life is illusory if accessible transportation is not available; hence most of Title II's provisions deal with transportation provided to the general public via bus, rail, taxis, and limousines. Aircraft are excluded.

All new public buses must be accessible to persons with disabilities. Transit authorities must provide supplementary or special services to those who cannot use fixed-route bus services. New over-the-road buses, new rail vehicles, and all new rail stations must be accessible. Existing rail systems must have one accessible car per train within the next five years.

How does this relate to your employment opportunities? In a 1986 Harris survey of 1,000 disabled people conducted for the International Center for the Disabled, prior to the ADA, 28 percent of the respondents said that a lack of accessible or affordable transportation was a major barrier to their employment. ADA's Title II and III address public transportation issues.

Title III: Public accommodations and services operated by private entities. Title II addresses government-operated public transportation. Title III requires public transportation operated by private entities such as bus and van companies to meet accessibility standards. Bus stations, for example, would fall under this provision.

Title III also prohibits discrimination against individuals with disabilities in the full and equal enjoyment of the goods, services, facilities, and

Figure 1-1   ADA Implementation Schedule

Title I. Employment

Employers of 25 or more people.	July 26, 1992.
Employers of 15 to 24 people.	July 26, 1994.
Employers of fewer than 15 people.	Law does not apply.

Title II. Transportation

Public transportation.	New stations built after January 26, 1992, must be accessible; one car per train must be accessible by July 26, 1995.
Rail transportation.	By July 26, 1995, Amtrak coaches must have one accessible car per train, and coaches must have some accessible seats; by July 26, 2000, coaches must have same number of accessible seats that they would have had if they had been built accessible.

Title III. Public Accommodations

Businesses with 25 or fewer employees and revenues of $1 million or less.	January 26, 1992.
Businesses with 10 or fewer employees and revenues of $500,000 or less.	January 26, 1993.

Title IV. Telecommunications

Telecommunications relay services to operate 24 hours a day.	July 26, 1993.

Title V. Miscellaneous

Effective dates of Title V.	Determined by analogous sections in Titles I through IV.

privileges of any place of public accommodation. Services for the disabled must be offered "in the most integrated setting appropriate to the needs of the individual," except when the individual poses a direct threat to the health or safety of others.

Public accommodations include a broad range of entities, from airports to zoos. It extends to sales, rental, and service establishments as well as to educational institutions, recreational facilities, and social service centers. Title III requires public accommodations to modify their policies and procedures and to provide auxiliary aids to disabled people unless doing so would fundamentally alter the nature of the organization or cause an undue burden.

All newly constructed and substantially renovated buildings must be readily accessible to people with disabilities. Existing facilities must be made accessible if changes are "readily achievable."

Title IV: Telecommunications. Title IV ensures that individuals with disabilities will be able to communicate electronically. It requires that, within three years, telephone companies must provide telecommunications relay services that enable hearing- and speech-impaired individuals to communicate with hearing individuals through the use of telecommunications devices for the deaf (TDD) and other nonvoice terminal devices. These services must be available around the clock, 365 days a year. Rates for telecommunications relay services must be no greater than rates for standard voice communication services.

Title IV also has implications for employment, as 23 percent of the respondents in the aforementioned Harris survey indicated that they did not have the equipment or adaptive devices needed to facilitate their work and to communicate with coworkers.

Title V: Miscellaneous provisions. In general, this title delineates the ADA's relationship to other laws, outlines insurance issues, and explains how each title in the act will be implemented. Most significantly, Title V prohibits retaliation against individuals who try to enforce their rights under the ADA.

Again, this relates to employment. If you already have a job and your employer is not living up to the ADA, you cannot be fired or in any way retaliated against for taking appropriate actions to bring your employer into compliance.

SCOPE OF TITLE I

Which Employers Are Regulated by ADA?

The Americans with Disabilities Act (ADA) ban on employment discrimination against people with disabilities applies to:

- Private employers
- Employment agencies
- Labor organizations
- Joint labor-management groups

As noted in the implementation schedule in Figure 1.1, Title I of the ADA currently applies to entities employing 25 or more people. In July of 1994, it will extend to employers of 15 or more people. Firms with fewer than 15 employees are exempt from coverage altogether.

An employer's size is determined by the number of workers employed at all of its business locations. If a company employs 50 people at its main office and 20 at a branch office, it has a total of 70 employees and is currently covered under Title I. It is important to know whether your employer is a chain operation like Wal-Mart or a franchise like 7-Eleven. A franchise is an independently owned business, so employer size is determined by the number of people working at a single location or at the locations owned by the same person.

Who Is Exempt from Title I Requirements?

Title I provisions do not apply to federal government agency employers, American Indian tribes, and tax-exempt private membership clubs. Religious organizations are allowed to hire members of their faith over other qualified applicants.

Who Is Protected?

Title I of the ADA prohibits discrimination in any terms or conditions of employment for "qualified individuals with disabilities." Employers must base their hiring decisions on an applicant's ability to perform the essential functions of a job, not on the person's disability. It also has a proactive requirement that employers must "reasonably accommodate" individuals with disabilities.

Who Are the Disabled?

As defined by the ADA, a disabled person is one who has a physical or mental impairment that substantially limits a major life activity, has a record of an impairment, or is regarded as having an impairment. Let's analyze each point in the definition.

1. Has a physical or mental impairment that substantially limits one or more major life activities. The term *impairment* includes any physiological disorder, cosmetic disfigurement, or anatomical loss as well as any mental or psychological disorder. While there is no inclusive list of impairments, the ADA does give examples such as: acquired immune deficiency syndrome (AIDS) and human immunodeficiency virus (HIV), alcoholism, cancer, cerebral palsy, diabetes, emotional illness, epilepsy, hearing and speech disorders, heart disease, certain learning disabilities such as dyslexia, mental retardation, muscular dystrophy, and visual impairments.

Some disabilities are obvious, others are not. This in no way affects an employer's obligations under the ADA, as long as the employer is aware of the disability.

Individuals who are currently abusing drugs or alcohol are not protected by the ADA. The act also excludes simple physical characteristics such as eye color, hair color, height, weight; sexual orientation such as homosexuality; and economic circumstances such as poverty. The ADA does not recognize transitory conditions such as pregnancy and broken bones, even though they may, for a time, substantially limit a major life activity.

A *major life activity* is a basic function such as caring for oneself, walking, talking, seeing, hearing, speaking, breathing, sitting, standing, lifting, reaching, and working. The term also includes cognitive functions such as learning, reasoning, and remembering.

With regard to the major life activity of working, the term *substantially limited* means that an individual is restricted in the ability to perform either a class of jobs or a broad range of jobs in various classes. The inability to perform a particular job is not a substantial limitation in the major life activity of working. It closes off only a single career path.

2. Has a record of impairment. This second prong of the definition protects people who had a disability in the past: for example, an individual with cancer in remission or a laborer with a history of back injuries. Anyone who has a past record of an impairment that restricts a major life activity is considered disabled even though the impairment does not currently cause a limitation. This includes rehabilitated drug addicts and recovering alcoholics.

One reason for covering people with a record of past impairment is to acknowledge that a person with a disabling condition does not cease to be disabled just because treatment alleviates the condition.

3. Is regarded as having an impairment. Also considered disabled are people who have no actual physical or mental impairment but who are viewed by others as disabled. An example is someone with a facial disfigurement. Although the person may not have any actual physical or mental limitations, the scars may create an impression of disability. That person cannot be discriminated against because of an employer's fear that customers will react negatively to the disfigured person's appearance. This provision attempts to keep irrational assumptions from entering into employment decisions. It also applies to people with hearing impairments, epilepsy, and other conditions that an employer may have misconceptions about.

Protection for Family and Friends

The ADA also provides some level of protection for people who care for relatives and friends with disabilities. It states that employers can't exclude or deny an equal job or benefits to qualified individuals because of a relationship or association—family, business, social, or other—with an individual who has a known disability. However, the employer does not have to supply an accommodation such as a modified work schedule—that requirement applies only to the person with the disability.

SITUATION ANALYSES

Situation No. 1

A parochial school wants to hire only teachers of its faith. Roger L. uses a wheelchair and does not practice the same religion as the school's administration. He's a highly qualified teacher in physical geography, a narrow specialty, and no other qualified teachers have applied for the job. During the job interview, Roger noticed no wheelchair access on the campus.

Can Roger use the ADA to compel the school to hire him? What will happen if he reports the school for failing to provide wheelchair access?

Analysis. No, Roger can't use the ADA to get the job.

This law upholds religious autonomy and clearly permits discrimination in employment based on religion. The school can reject Roger because his beliefs are inconsistent with the school's.

If Roger can prove that he was rejected because of his disability (as by the hiring of someone with other religious beliefs and no disability), the school would lose this defense. This exception to the ADA pertains only to religious organizations and only to employment.

Roger's charge of access discrimination will be well received by federal, state, and local agencies. The mandates clearly apply to private schools and colleges. He might even qualify for compensation because of this violation.

Situation No. 2

Connie P. is a nurse. She had a laryngectomy and uses a hand-held electronic voice box. She has applied for a promotion to a nursing supervisor position.

The hospital refuses to promote Connie because the union contract states that promotions must be given only to employees who are "able to fully perform all functions of the job." A nursing supervisor must be able to use the hospital paging system for emergencies. One of Connie's nondisabled coworkers with less experience wants the job.

Can Connie use the ADA as a basis for convincing the employer to ignore the contract? Can she enforce her right to a promotion if it refuses? Must she research workplace alternatives herself?

Analysis. Connie can credibly argue that the ADA preempts the collective bargaining agreement. Even specific job duties written into the contract will be construed liberally in her favor. Only essential duties are likely to survive government or court scrutiny. That means Connie can enforce her right to the promotion if some practical solution ("reasonable accommodation") to the paging problem can be found.

Connie has no legal duty to research the matter, but doing so would increase her chances of successfully confronting the employer. She should consult with her union official and follow the contract grievance procedure.

The many bells, whistles, and lights available for paging should convince the hospital to promote Connie forthwith.

Situation No. 3

Sharon J. is a nondisabled manager who witnessed discrimination against another manager confined to a wheelchair. When a charge of discrimination was filed, the Equal Employment Opportunity Commission (EEOC) contacted Sharon to assist with its investigation. The company policy manual states that managers are expected to protect its interests at all times.

Sharon wants to cooperate with the EEOC but fears retaliation by her employer. Is there any protection for her? Does it prevent mistreatment on the job as well as termination?

Analysis. Yes, Sharon is fully protected against any retaliation on the job.

It is unlawful for an employer to take negative action against someone who participates in an investigation of discriminatory practices. It makes no difference whether or not they actually occurred.

Sharon is even protected if she just states her opposition to such practices. But, as a manager, she is in an excellent position to do something positive about the discrimination.

Discrimination is often the result of insensitivity or ignorance. Why doesn't Sharon suggest a management meeting to discuss the issue? The local EEOC or state rehabilitation agency might be able to provide a guest speaker at no charge. She could circulate a copy of my earlier book, *Complying with the ADA: A Small Business Guide to Hiring and Employing the Disabled.* Or she could draft a policy on accommodating disabled employees. Maybe she could suggest a few workplace alterations so other people with disabilities could be hired.

Situation No. 4

Peter C. is a technical writer who was fired from his last job because of chronic alcohol abuse (prior to enactment of the ADA). He didn't disclose the reasons for his termination in applying for employment at his present job.

Now Peter is late to work and absent often. He wants to speak with the human resources manager to seek treatment. However, he is concerned that he will lose his job again by disclosing his problem.

Does the ADA protect Peter? Must he accept the human resources manager's recommendation? If he needs to take time off for rehabilitation, is the employer required to grant it? With pay?

Analysis. Surprisingly, Peter is entitled to some protection under the ADA. Unlike someone who uses illegal (or nonprescribed regulated) drugs, he can't be discharged merely for alcohol abuse.

But the protection ends there. If Peter is excessively late, absent, or performs poorly, he can lose his job like any other employee.

Peter is under no obligation to accept the human resources manager's recommendation. But he has taken the first step by recognizing his problem.

The employer is not required to give Peter time off to recover. Therefore, no pay is required either. Only a company policy to give him the time (with or without pay) will help.

CHAPTER TWO

From Hiring to Firing: Employment Practices Regulated under Title I

IN WHAT AREAS OF EMPLOYMENT IS DISCRIMINATION PROHIBITED?

An employer may not discriminate against a qualified individual with a disability in any part of the employment process. The Americans with Disabilities Act (ADA) specifically mentions the following areas:

- Job application procedures: recruiting, advertising, and processing of applications.
- Hiring, upgrading, promotion, tenure, demotion, transfer, layoff, termination, right of return from layoff, and rehiring.
- Rates of pay and other forms of compensation.
- Job assignments, job classifications, organizational structures, position descriptions, lines of progression, and seniority lists.
- Leaves of absence, sick leave, and other leaves.
- Fringe benefits, whether or not they are administered by the employer.
- Training, including apprenticeships, professional meetings, and related activities.
- Employer-sponsored activities, including social or recreational programs.

As with other civil rights laws prohibiting discrimination in employment, the ADA does not negate an employer's right to choose and maintain a qualified work force. If you are applying for a job that requires lifting 50-pound boxes, the employer can test you to determine whether you can lift those boxes. If you want a job as a typist, you will have to take a typing test.

WHAT CONSTITUTES EMPLOYER DISCRIMINATION?

The ADA prohibits several specific forms of discrimination in dealing with job applicants and employees with disabilities. These include:

1. Limiting, segregating, or classifying people with disabilities in a way that limits their opportunities or status. Employers cannot make assumptions about what a class of individuals with disabilities can or cannot do. They cannot maintain separate lines of promotion, different pay scales, or limited benefits for employees with disabilities. They cannot restrict them from performing certain tasks that are essential to their position.

Example _____

XYZ Corporation has a separate job category for janitors with developmental disabilities, a category with lower pay and no benefits or seniority rights even though their duties are the same as other janitors. This policy violates Title I of the ADA.

Employment activities must take place in an integrated manner. This means that employees with disabilities must not be segregated into particular work areas. Amenities must also be integrated.

Example _____

If your company's existing coffee-break room is inaccessible to employees who use wheelchairs, a comparable area must be made available. The alternative room does not have to be the same size as long as it is comparably equipped.

2. Entering into discriminatory third-party contracts. Employers must keep employees with disabilities in mind when entering into any contractual relationship such as collective bargaining agreements with unions, employment agency referrals, contracts with hotels for seminars or workshops, and contracts with consultants. If your employer contracts with a hotel to hold a staff training program, the employer must ensure that the location is accessible for all employees.

3. Denying health insurance coverage to an individual with a disability. All people with disabilities are entitled to equal access to all fringe benefits the employer provides, including any health insurance coverage. Employers may not refuse a job to a person with disabilities just because the company's insurance plan does not cover a particular disability or because of an anticipated increase in insurance costs. Employers also may not deny health insurance coverage to an employee based on a disability.

However, the law does not require that all medical conditions be covered. An employer can still offer insurance policies that limit coverage for certain procedures or treatments, such as a limit on the number of X-rays, or noncoverage of experimental procedures. Employers may also continue to offer policies that contain exclusions for preexisting conditions and certain types of claims such as psychological counseling or alcoholism, even though such exclusions might adversely affect people with disabilities. Coverage cannot be denied for illnesses unrelated to the preexisting condition.

Example ———————————————————————————

A new employee who has diabetes before starting on a job must be given the same health insurance coverage as other employees. If the company's plan denies coverage for preexisting medical problems, the new employee's medical expenses for diabetes would not be covered. If the employee later has medical claims based upon cancer that was diagnosed *after* the beginning of employment, the cancer-related claims would be covered, assuming cancer is not excluded from coverage.

4. Discriminating against a qualified individual on the basis of that person's relationship or association with a disabled individual. As noted in Chapter 1, this provision extends beyond family associations. A qualified individual cannot be denied employment because a roommate has acquired immune deficiency syndrome (AIDS) or a spouse has cancer. The employer, however, has no affirmative obligation to provide released time from work or other accommodations.

5. Using tests that screen out people with disabilities. Employers may administer only those tests that reflect essential job requirements and the applicant's skills rather than his or her impairments. Any selection criteria that automatically screen out people with disabilities are prohibited.

Example ———————————————————————————

Mr. Stutts, who is dyslexic, was denied the job of heavy equipment operator because he could not pass a written test used by the employer to enter a training program that is a prerequisite for the job. The question to be answered here is whether the written test for the training program is a necessary criterion for the job of heavy equipment operator. If it is, the question becomes whether a reasonable accommodation such as an oral test or a reader could be provided to ensure that the test reflects the applicant's job skills rather than his impaired ability to read.

6. *Upholding discriminatory employment standards.* Like Title VII of the Civil Rights Act of 1964, the ADA prohibits both intentional and unintentional discrimination. A seemingly benign practice that has a disparate impact on disabled employees, such as requiring all employees to have a valid driver's license, could be challenged under the ADA. Under Equal Employment Opportunity Commission regulations, however, certain policies that are uniformly applied may not be challenged under the disparate impact theory.

Example _____

Your company has a policy that employees are not eligible for a leave of absence during the first six months on the job. Although this policy may have a disparate impact on employees with disabilities, it cannot be challenged under the ADA.

7. *Failing to make reasonable accommodations.* Employers must act affirmatively to restructure their organization of work to expand opportunities to disabled applicants and employees. This involves making reasonable accommodations to the known physical or mental limitations of an otherwise qualified individual with a disability unless the accommodation would impose an undue hardship on the operation of the business. "Reasonable accommodation" is a central concept in the ADA that touches on provisions in every title. It is discussed at length in Chapter 12.

8. *Conducting discriminatory medical examinations or inquiries.* The ADA identifies the types of tests, inquiries, and examinations that are allowable at different junctures in the hiring process so that qualified applicants with disabilities are not screened out unfairly. Figure 2.1 summarizes the types of inquiries that can be made at different junctures in the hiring process.

Medical examinations are not permitted at the preemployment phase in the hiring process. During this period, employers may not make *any* inquiries about disabilities, absenteeism, illness, or worker's compensation history. That includes job applications, interviews, and reference checks. They can ask questions about your ability to perform job-related functions,

Figure 2.1   Preemployment Tests at a Glance

Preoffer Qualification Test	Postoffer Medical Evaluation
Evaluates functional capacity to do the job.	Evaluates physical or mental health status.
Permitted prior to job offer.	Permitted only following offer. Employment may be contingent on passing.
Test must be job related.	Evaluation need not be job related. Mandatory postemployment evaluation must be job related and consistent with business necessity.
Exclusionary criteria must not tend to screen out individuals with disabilities unless job related and consistent with business necessity.	Exclusionary criteria must not tend to screen out individuals with disabilities unless job related and consistent with business necessity.
Assuming the above is true, an applicant may be denied a job based on failing a qualification test related to an essential job function only if the applicant cannot perform the essential job function or pass the qualification test with a reasonable accommodation.	Assuming the above is true, a job offer may be withdrawn based on evaluation results that indicate inability to meet employment criteria or if there is imminent risk of direct threat to self or others, based on current status.
Formal qualification tests must be the same for all. The employer may ask an applicant with a disability to describe or demonstrate the performance of a job function only if it appears that a known disability may interfere.	Medical tests and questions must be the same for all.
Actual decision whether or not to offer the job is employer's responsibility.	Actual decision whether or not to begin employment is employer's responsibility.

Source: Reprinted with permission from *The ADA: A Compliance Seminar* (manual). Long Grove, Ill.: Kemper Risk Management Services, 1992.

but they cannot ask questions about your disability in and of itself. More about this in Chapter 8.

Example _____

In hiring drivers to deliver pizzas, an employer may ask whether an applicant has a driver's license but not whether the applicant has a visual disability.

The only legitimate purpose of a medical examination under the ADA is to determine if an applicant can perform specific job functions, not to determine if the person has a disability. After an offer of employment is made, employers may require you to take a medical examination and condition their offer on the results—as long as *all* new employees are required to take such an examination.

All medical records must be kept confidential and released only on a need-to-know basis. Government officials investigating compliance complaints must be given information on request; managers may be given information regarding accommodations and work restrictions; safety personnel may be given information relative to emergency treatment.

Once a person is on the job, an employer cannot require a medical examination or inquire about a disability unless it is job-related and consistent with business necessity.

Example _____

Your boss notices that you have been losing your hair and looking tired, so he asks you to undergo a medical exam for cancer within the next month. He is in violation of Title I of the ADA.

Example _____

Federal safety regulations require bus and truck drivers to have a medical examination at least biennially. The Occupational Safety and Health Administration (OSHA) lead standard requires that employees exposed to lead be tested periodically to determine the blood lead levels. These job-related medical tests are allowed under Title I.

Regarding drug testing, nothing in the ADA prohibits employers from testing applicants or employees for the presence of illegal drugs. Employers may refuse to hire an applicant or may discipline an employee if tests detect illegal drug use. The term *illegal drug* does not include drugs taken under medical supervision, even experimental drugs. An employer is not required to provide a rehabilitation program as a reasonable accommodation for a current drug user, but many companies have instituted employee assistance programs. They have found that it is more cost-effective to rehabilitate qualified employees than to terminate them.

EMPLOYER DEFENSES

Business Necessity

An employer may defend a practice that discriminates against a qualified individual with a disability if the practice is job-related and consistent with business necessity.

Direct Threat to Health or Safety

Direct threat is defined as "a *significant* risk to the health or safety of others that cannot be eliminated with reasonable accommodation." Decisions in this regard cannot be based on generalizations or irrational fears about the disability. They must rest on the facts of the individual case. It is not the applicant's or employee's responsibility to prove that he or she does not pose a risk in the workplace.

Example ──

> In the case of the *School Board of Nassau County v. Arline*, it was found that Arline was qualified to be an elementary school teacher even during the period when she had an active case of tuberculosis. The medical evidence showed that once a person with tuberculosis has begun antibiotic treatment, the chance of infecting others is quite low.[1]

Risk of Injury

This is a legitimate concern. If a worker's disability causes an accident on the job or a job-related illness, an employer's insurance coverage and worker's compensation costs could increase substantially. A customer or coworker who is injured as a result of an employee's disability could even bring a negligent hiring lawsuit against an employer who placed that person in a dangerous job without ensuring that he or she could do the work safely. On the other hand, denying employment to people with disabilities because they *might* cause accidents or have more frequent insurance claims is disability-based employment discrimination. As with direct

---

[1]*School Board of Nassau County v. Arline*, 480 U.S. 273, 43 Fair Empl. Prac. Cas. 81 (1987).

threats to health and safety, there must be not just an *elevated* risk of future injury but a *probability of substantial harm*.

Example _____

A railroad company's rules provided that any welder with epilepsy could not remain on the job. A worker who acquired epilepsy from an injury in an auto accident was discharged in accordance with company rules. The Supreme Court of Wisconsin held that the company rule was unreasonable because it was applied without first finding a reasonable probability of serious future harm. Medical testimony showed that the worker had never had an on-the-job seizure and had suffered no seizures since being placed on medication.

Food Service Workers

State and local public health departments are on the front lines of protecting the public health. These legitimate laws and regulations are not preempted by the ADA. The ADA requires the secretary of health and human services to use valid scientific evidence to determine which diseases are transmitted through the handling of food and then to issue an annually updated list of such diseases. The list includes common diseases such as hepatitis A, streptococcal and salmonellal infections, as well as lesser known infections. AIDS and the human immunodeficiency virus (HIV) are not included on the list.

If an individual has a communicable disease that can be transmitted through the handling of food, and if the risk of the disease being transmitted on the job cannot be eliminated by reasonable accommodation, an employer may refuse to hire an individual in a food handling job.

Example _____

John, a carpenter, has an infectious disease that can be cured by taking medication for a specified period of time. His employer must make the reasonable accommodation of allowing him time off to take the medication unless that would impose an undue hardship on the operation of the business.

What about AIDS?

Under the ADA, job applicants and employees with HIV, AIDS-related complex, or AIDS must be treated the same as other individuals with a disability. They cannot be excluded from food service jobs, health care jobs, or jobs that involve close contact with children.

SITUATION ANALYSES

Situation No. 1

Maria D. has been asked to attend her company's convention in another state. She has learned that the hotel doesn't have wheelchair access. The only way she can attend is to be carried around by two people.

Does the ADA cover Maria in this situation? How should she approach her employer about the access issue?

Analysis. Maria is definitely covered in this situation. Even if a meeting planner or other outside contractor is arranging the convention for the employer, ADA regulations fully apply. The employer has a duty to require compliance by the hotel and by all transportation, meeting, lodging, and eating facilities connected with the event.

Because the hotel (and other entities used during the trip) must comply with the ADA anyway, Maria might suggest that her employer use this as a reason to change locations. The employer will then be "on notice" that it is participating in violation of a potent federal law.

It may not be pleasant for Maria, but just think of how she would feel about missing the conference or having to be carried in.

Situation No. 2

Norma R. contracted tuberculosis (an infectious disease) after working for three years as an accountant. She needs to take a month off to recover during the busiest time of the year.

Must the employer give her the time off? Must she be paid her regular salary for the time?

Analysis. If the ADA is the only law that applies, the answer is no to both questions. The sick leave or personal leave policy of the employer will determine Norma's right to return to work. Otherwise, only a state or local law (or written employment agreement) would give her reemployment rights.

The employer is also under no obligation to pay Norma. Any rights she has would also be pursuant to a law or employment agreement. She might also be eligible for state or private disability insurance benefits.

Employers are given great latitude with regard to preventing the spread of infectious diseases. The basic ADA approach is to allow all "reasonable" precautions to prevent the disease from being transmitted to employees and others contacted on the job.

Situation No. 3

Fred A.'s wife is HIV positive and terminally ill. He mentioned this during his interview for corporate counsel and nothing further was said. The following day he received a call from the interviewer offering him the job contingent on passing a physical examination. The employer does not routinely conduct preemployment physicals.

Must Fred consent to the physical? Can the offer be revoked if he is found to be HIV positive? What if he is not?

Analysis. Fred might argue that he is the victim of discrimination because of "disparate treatment"—other applicants were not required to take a physical. This is a weak argument, though, because the ADA (and related law) appears to permit employer discretion regarding preemployment medical examinations.

The offer can't be withdrawn whether Fred is HIV positive or not. The ADA prohibits discrimination against job applicants because of a "known disability of an individual with whom the qualified individual is known to have a family, business, or social relationship or association." This long phrase clearly protects Fred.

If being HIV positive presented a significant risk to the health or safety of other employees, the result might be different. It doesn't, though, and it also doesn't interfere with Fred's ability to perform corporate counsel duties.

CHAPTER THREE

Where the Jobs Are

Although workplace attitudes toward people with disabilities are changing, the unemployment rate among the job-aged disabled population is more than 60 percent, as compared with less than 10 percent among the general population. Two out of three people with disabilities are not working. And of those, two out of three *want* to work. With roughly $200 billion in benefits being paid out each year to nonworking people with disabilities, it just doesn't make sense for businesses to say they can't afford to accommodate people with disabilities.

This chapter looks at some promising career fields for the twenty-first century and the skills that will be needed to succeed. The information here is taken from the U.S. Department of Labor's *Occupational Outlook Quarterly* and *Monthly Labor Review* and from Carol Kleiman's excellent book, *The 100 Best Jobs for the 1990s and Beyond.*

If you haven't settled on a career field because you're not sure what's out there, the Department of Labor's Bureau of Labor Statistics (BLS) publishes a lot of helpful career information, and many of its materials have been recorded for the blind. The following three publications are considered to be the bibles for labor market research:

1. The *Guide for Occupational Exploration* is a user-friendly reference work written in nontechnical language. It divides the world of work into 12 major interest areas, which are divided into 66 work groups, and then into subgroups with specific job titles.

2. The *Occupational Outlook Handbook* offers full-length descriptions of some 200 jobs, with an outline of working conditions, salary data, and growth projections.
3. The *Dictionary of Occupational Titles* is self-explanatory.

These publications are widely available in libraries, or they can be purchased through the BLS Chicago sales office (312/353-1880). The Bureau of Labor Statistics also conducts and publishes many wage and salary surveys, another area worth studying before you begin your job search. The Bureau of Labor Statistics has nine regional offices around the country.

A CHANGING WORK FORCE

The passage of the Americans with Disabilities Act (ADA) in 1990 coincides with far-reaching changes in the U.S. labor market—changes that are, for the most part, positive for people who are physically challenged in earning a living. The most significant trend, according to the U.S. Department of Labor, is a projected labor shortage.

• Only 15 percent of new entrants to the work force will be white men. Women, immigrants, and groups that are now considered minorities will account for more than 80 percent of the U.S. labor force growth in the year 2000.
• The labor force wil grow at a rate of only 1.2 percent in the year 2000, compared with a annual growth rate of 2.6 percent in the 1970s. In 1995, the number of Americans 18 to 24 years of age will bottom out to a little under 24 million, compared with a peak of 30 million in 1980.
• One out of three people will be 50 years of age or older by the turn of the century. Most workers will be between 35 and 54 years of age.

These changes mean that businesses will be actively recruiting previously underutilized segments of the labor force. Skilled workers—regardless of age, sex, race, national origin, or disability—will be in great demand. And the unique needs of this new work force will have to be accommodated, not as a moral imperative, but as a business necessity.

CHANGING NATURE OF WORK

A shrinking labor market and the passage of the ADA open doors to new employment opportunities for disabled Americans, but you still have to know where to knock. Although your disability might shape your career choices, you could be surprised to find that certain jobs that were closed to you in the past are now viable career options, thanks to new technologies.

Many of the trends that will affect your job in the 1990s are already in place:

• By the twenty-first century, 90 percent of the 21 million jobs expected to be created will be in the service sector of the economy. Service jobs will not pay as well as the blue-collar jobs they're replacing, so annual incomes and the standard of living of U.S. workers will decline.

• Manufacturing jobs, which once accounted for more than 75 percent of all U.S. jobs, today account for less than 20 percent. Of the 12 million new jobs added to the economy between 1985 and 1990, fewer than 1 million were in manufacturing. The rest were in the service sector.

• By the year 2000, three out of every four workers currently employed will need retraining for the new jobs of the next century.

• Specialty niche occupations such as bookkeepers, stenographers, word processors, and administrative assistants will give way to jobs with broader responsibilities.

• American job seekers will be competing in a global economy. Businesses will actively recruit trained workers from all over the world.

WORKPLACE OF THE TWENTY-FIRST CENTURY

New technologies are changing how work is done, where it is done, and what types of skills are needed to do it.

Advances in telecommunications are enabling more and more people to work from their homes, linked by computers, modems, fax machines, and telephone-answering devices. The Electronics Industries Association reports that in 1991 some 30 million households were part of the home office phenomenon. This is good news for people with mobility problems. However, corporate downsizing, layoffs, and mergers means that fewer people are doing more work. The pattern emerging is one of working fewer hours in the office but more hours from home.

To tap into new sources of qualified labor, corporations will have to offer work-at-home options, flexible hours, job sharing, cafeteria benefit plans, and even child care. In fact, various flexible scheduling arrangements were already in place at 54 percent of the 450 companies participating in a recent study conducted by Hewitt Associates.

Virtually every occupation will be revolutionized by new technology. "Computer literacy is becoming a basic job requirement," says Steve Cole, a database consultant for the Blue Cross/Blue Shield Association. "Everyone entering the job market today—white- and blue-collar workers alike—will be using computers at some point in their working life. You won't have to be a computer programmer, but you will have to know how to input data and obtain information from computers to do your job. You may not even need keyboard skills as the number of input devices continues to multiply."

There are 34 subsidized computer training and placement programs for people with disabilities across the country, cosponsored by the state departments of rehabilitation services, IBM, local community groups, and area businesses.

There are also a growing number of places like the TAAD Center (Technological Aids and Assistance for the Disabled) in Chicago, where you can try out various kinds of adaptive equipment free of charge. Staff members help clients learn which tools are right for them, refer them to the best places to purchase adaptive tools, and provide support in learning to use these tools.

Brains will be more important than brawn in the workplace of the twenty-first century. A college degree or technical or vocational training—some credentials beyond high school—will be a prerequisite for most jobs with a future. Also important are associate degrees, certificates of vocational and trade school training, and continuing education credits. The U.S. apprenticeship system is expanding to include service jobs such as child care provider, computer programmer, veterinary technician, chef, paramedic, and others. In the 1980s, a master of business administration degree was a ticket to the fast track. Today, a good liberal arts education is becoming the degree of choice for more and more employers.

TOP CAREER FIELDS FOR YEAR 2000

The U.S. economy is divided into two broad sectors: service producing and goods producing. The service-producing sector will create four out of five of all new jobs by the year 2000. This grouping includes transportation, communications, public utilities, wholesale and retail trade, finance, insurance, real estate, government, and social services.

• *Engineering and computer technology.* This category of jobs is on the cutting edge of change. Workers in these fields will help determine how successful the United States will be in a competitive global economy. The hottest occupations right now are computer-related technical jobs, which are projected to grow by more than 70 percent by the year 2000. The engineer will be the number one professional in demand. Other growth occupations in this field include: computer graphics—CAD/CAM and CAI specialists (computer-aided design, manufacturing, and imaging)—computer operator, computer programmer, computer systems analyst, and database manager.

• ***Business and financial services.*** According to the U.S. Department of Labor, this is the fastest growing segment of the service-producing sector, with some 3.3 million jobs expected to open up over the next decade. The paralegal is the fastest growing semiprofessional job in this category.

• ***Health care.*** This field, which is expected to add some 3.2 million jobs over the next 10 years, includes more of the best paying and fastest growing jobs than any other occupational category. Of the 10 fastest growing occupations in the United States, 6 are in health care: licensed practical nurse, occupational therapist, physical therapist, physician's assistant, radiologic technologist, and registered nurse.

• ***Information technology.*** Trend-watcher John Naisbitt has dubbed this "the information age." Demand for workers who can manipulate and analyze data will increase. Advances in microelectronics, fiber optics, and digital technology will create jobs in storage, retrieval, analysis, and transmittal of information. Telecommunications will be one of the fastest growing fields in the 1990s.

• ***Biotechnology and science.*** Scientists are already in short supply, and the demand is becoming more urgent, especially for scientists who specialize in genetic engineering, the environment, and outer space. Carol Kleiman calls this field "the new frontier of the next century."

• ***Lasers.*** Lasers are already being used in myriad ways: to perform microsurgery, to speed up communication through fiber optics, to align underground pipes, and to expedite the printing process. As the use of lasers continues to expand, so, too, will the demand for medical staff trained in laser medicine and for laser specialists to work in communications and manufacturing.

SHRINKING CAREER SECTORS

The goods-producing sector, which includes agriculture, forestry, fishing, mining, manufacturing, and construction, is shrinking. The only industry in this group that is expected to show any significant expansion in job opportunities is construction.

• ***Manufacturing and repair.*** More than half of the 30 occupations on the Bureau of Labor Statistics list of declining occupations are in manufacturing.

• ***Business and office.*** While office automation is creating jobs for some, it is pulling the rug out from under others such as bookkeepers, accountants, and auditing clerks. Typists and word processors are also on the down curve.

• **_Agriculture._** Advanced technology and larger machinery used in crop and livestock production will mean fewer jobs for farm workers.

Figures 3.1 and 3.2 show a more complete tally of growing and declining job fields.

THINK SMALL

Don't limit your job search to Fortune 500 companies. With large corporations continuing to downsize, most new employment in the United States in the 1990s will be generated by businesses with fewer than 50 employees. Although large corporations can offer higher salaries and more lavish benefit packages, workers in smaller firms generally have more job satisfaction, greater opportunity for advancement, more sense of teamwork and camaraderie on the job, and more control over their work environment.

THINK ALTERNATIVELY

The more you know about the job market, the more realistic you can be in your choice. If your first career choice is not open to you because of your disability, think alternatively.

With the thousands of jobs available today, it's hard to know which paths make sense unless you group the choices in some way. Most career counselors use a system of career clusters and job families to help their clients identify a realm of possibilities rather than a single job. Communications, for instance, is a _career cluster._ Within it are the _job families_ of printing and publishing, broadcast communications, design, and graphic arts, to name a few.

All jobseekers can benefit from this clustering system, but it is most helpful for people with disabilities who want to explore a realm of career options within a chosen field. If you have a speech difficulty, for instance, you may never get to be an on-air newscaster, but you might well become a news producer, researcher, reporter, or editor—someone who shapes the news outside of the limelight.

Thinking alternatively paid off for Greg Gizewski, a quadriplegic who holds college degrees in journalism and art. "I initially wanted to go into architecture, but to manipulate the existing tools—a T square and a compass—you have to have fine finger movement. I can't move my fingers even with a brace, so it wasn't feasible for me to go into that field." Today Greg works as a computer-aided design specialist at Safety-Kleen, a major chemical recycling company outside of Chicago.

Figure 3.1   Fastest Growing Occupations

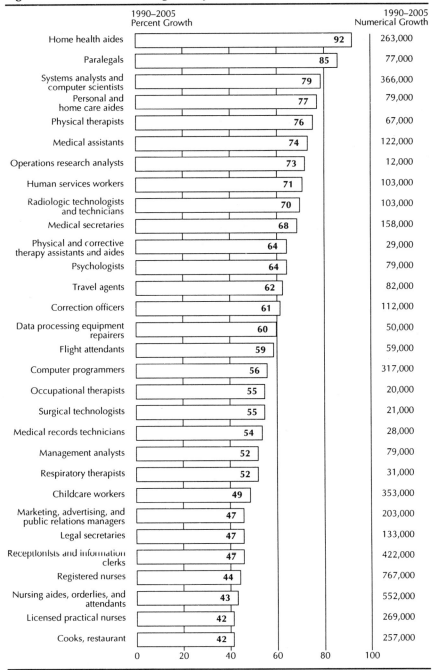

	1990–2005 Percent Growth	1990–2005 Numerical Growth
Home health aides	92	263,000
Paralegals	85	77,000
Systems analysts and computer scientists	79	366,000
Personal and home care aides	77	79,000
Physical therapists	76	67,000
Medical assistants	74	122,000
Operations research analysts	73	12,000
Human services workers	71	103,000
Radiologic technologists and technicians	70	103,000
Medical secretaries	68	158,000
Physical and corrective therapy assistants and aides	64	29,000
Psychologists	64	79,000
Travel agents	62	82,000
Correction officers	61	112,000
Data processing equipment repairers	60	50,000
Flight attendants	59	59,000
Computer programmers	56	317,000
Occupational therapists	55	20,000
Surgical technologists	55	21,000
Medical records technicians	54	28,000
Management analysts	52	79,000
Respiratory therapists	52	31,000
Childcare workers	49	353,000
Marketing, advertising, and public relations managers	47	203,000
Legal secretaries	47	133,000
Receptionists and information clerks	47	422,000
Registered nurses	44	767,000
Nursing aides, orderlies, and attendants	43	552,000
Licensed practical nurses	42	269,000
Cooks, restaurant	42	257,000

Source: U.S. Department of Labor, "Outlook: 1990–2005," *Occupational Outlook Quarterly*, Fall 1991.

Figure 3.2 Occupations Losing Workers

Shrinking occupations are projected by the *number of job openings*, rather than by the rate of decline. Many occupations with the fastest rates of decline are small in size, resulting in employment declines that aren't very significant.

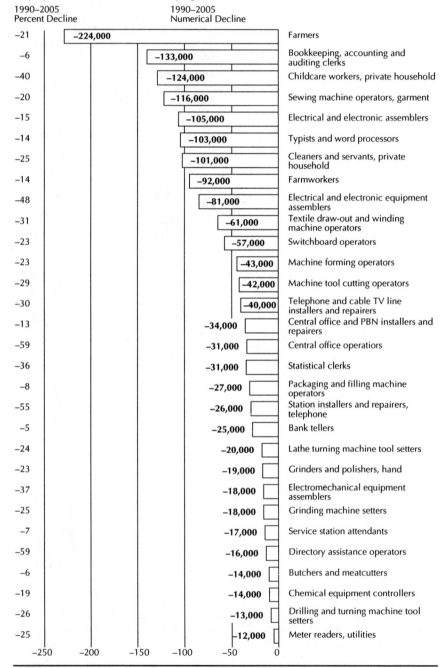

1990–2005 Percent Decline	1990–2005 Numerical Decline	
−21	−224,000	Farmers
−6	−133,000	Bookkeeping, accounting and auditing clerks
−40	−124,000	Childcare workers, private household
−20	−116,000	Sewing machine operators, garment
−15	−105,000	Electrical and electronic assemblers
−14	−103,000	Typists and word processors
−25	−101,000	Cleaners and servants, private household
−14	−92,000	Farmworkers
−48	−81,000	Electrical and electronic equipment assemblers
−31	−61,000	Textile draw-out and winding machine operators
−23	−57,000	Switchboard operators
−23	−43,000	Machine forming operators
−29	−42,000	Machine tool cutting operators
−30	−40,000	Telephone and cable TV line installers and repairers
−13	−34,000	Central office and PBN installers and repairers
−59	−31,000	Central office operatiors
−36	−31,000	Statistical clerks
−8	−27,000	Packaging and filling machine operators
−55	−26,000	Station installers and repairers, telephone
−5	−25,000	Bank tellers
−24	−20,000	Lathe turning machine tool setters
−23	−19,000	Grinders and polishers, hand
−37	−18,000	Electromechanical equipment assemblers
−25	−18,000	Grinding machine setters
−7	−17,000	Service station attendants
−59	−16,000	Directory assistance operators
−6	−14,000	Butchers and meatcutters
−19	−14,000	Chemical equipment controllers
−26	−13,000	Drilling and turning machine tool setters
−25	−12,000	Meter readers, utilities

−250   −200   −150   −100   −50   0

Source: U.S. Department of Labor, "Outlook: 1990–2005," *Occupational Outlook Quarterly*, Fall 1991.

LEARN TO SPOT EMPLOYMENT TRENDS

Both the *New York Times* and the *Washington Post* publish annual or semi-annual supplements on employment trends, technology in the workplace, and labor force retraining efforts. The business section of Tuesday's *New York Times* carries a careers column, and the business section of the Sunday edition contains a page entitled "What's New in . . . ," which reports on trends in different fields. "Labor Letter" is a regular feature in Tuesday's *Wall Street Journal*, reporting on "People and Their Jobs in Offices, Fields and Factories." Even *Women's Wear Daily* carries a thrice-weekly column called "From Where I Sit," which discusses career issues. Long-time career columnists like Joyce Lain Kennedy and Carol Kleiman are syndicated nationally.

BE FLEXIBLE

The American economy is no longer one in which most of us are employed by monolithic manufacturing corporations. Instead, ours is a service-producing economy in which workers using new technologies can complete tasks in record time.

The key to survival in this high-tech information society is adaptability—a willingness to learn new skills, to accept changes in the way work is done, and to explore new career opportunities. For people who are physically or mentally challenged, adaptability is a way of life.

SITUATION ANALYSES

Situation No. 1

Burton F. is a recent college graduate who just became a certified public accountant. He is a qualified entry-level accountant who graduated with honors, but a serious accident prevented him from attending a recognized university. His studies were done through extension and correspondence programs.

Burton applies for a job with a major accounting firm. The firm requires graduation from a list of prestigious business schools for all entry-level accountants. Must it make an exception for Burton? Must it change its policy because the policy discriminates against applicants with disabilities?

Analysis. No to both questions.

Because he lacks the required business school credentials, Burton is not "otherwise qualified" under the ADA definition. Graduation from a prestigious business school may be an arbitrary, unnecessary, and even goofy requirement, but as long as it's applied equally to all applicants, it is perfectly legal. There's no law against poor business judgment—even for accountants.

Situation No. 2

Roberta B. applies for an engineering job. The interviewer says she would be working on a high-priority project that might require her to be on the job every day for the next six weeks. She says this is acceptable.

The interviewer offers her the job conditioned on her passing a physical examination. Unfortunately, the physical exam shows that she has high blood pressure, and the doctor writes an opinion that she should not work the long hours required by the job.

Must the employer hire Roberta because she is "otherwise qualified" for the job? Must it make a reasonable accommodation to her disability?

Analysis. The employer is under no duty to hire Roberta in any job.

If a normal work schedule was involved, her high blood pressure would probably not be a legitimate medical concern. In that case, the disability could not be used to prevent her employment.

A reasonable accommodation of fewer work days or shorter hours would create an undue hardship for the employer. Hiring Roberta under the working conditions required would present an undue risk to her safety as well.

Situation No. 3

Elena K. applies for a job as a programmer. She is highly skilled, but because she is blind in one eye, she tends to become fatigued if she works at a keyboard for more than an hour.

The application form lists several disabilities and asks the applicant to check the ones that apply. One is "blindness," but Elena doesn't check it. A few days later, she is invited for an interview.

When the interviewer notices her glass eye, he asks her to sit at a computer and demonstrate that she can program it.

Can the employer refuse to hire Elena because she didn't check blindness on the application? Can it require her to pass the impromptu programming test?

Analysis. Assuming Elena is otherwise qualified, that job is hers. Both the employer and the interviewer have violated the ADA.

Under the ADA, employers are specifically prohibited from using disability checklists on employment applications, so Elena is under no obligation to incriminate herself. I would advise her to avoid answering any variation of a checklist that requires disclosure of non-job-related disabilities (even though it might also include job-related ones).

The interviewer violated the ADA, too. Preemployment tests can't be selectively administered to applicants with disabilities. He should have merely asked Elena if she needed any accommodation.

CHAPTER FOUR

Self-Assessment: Matching Your Skills with Essential Job Functions

There are many promising career paths for the 1990s, but which ones are right for you? Before you answer that question, make sure your response isn't dictated by what others have told you are "good" careers for people with your disability. Each day we hear about a person with some disability successfully performing a job that would have been closed to him or her a generation ago. Don't allow someone else to limit your career horizons. Before you decide to take a position, ask yourself, Is this the right job for me?

PREPARING YOUR PERSONAL INVENTORY

If you've analyzed the current job market using some of the information and resources in the preceding chapter, you can now take a look at what marketable skills, interests, and experiences you have to offer. Until you go through the process of discovering who you are and what you want, you're not ready to select a career. The following questions will give you a basic framework for self-analysis.

- What do I want out of a job?
- What are my interests?
- What are my skills?
- What are my areas of professional experience?

Let's take a closer look at these points to construct a framework for self-analysis.

Analyze Your Work Values

Noted careers journalist Melanie Astaire Witt has developed a work values survey to help job seekers identify what they want out of a job (Figure 4.1). This kind of exercise can help you understand what trade-offs you are willing to make in your work life. For instance, although a person with a visual impairment might enjoy working with other people, a job that offers a work-at-home option might be more viable. Or perhaps a high salary isn't as important as a flexible schedule. You get the idea.

Analyze Your Interests

We do best what we like most—it's human nature. Our interests cannot always be parlayed into paid work, but sometimes they can be—if you take the time to think about how they might relate to actual job demands. Do you enjoy music or play an instrument? Are you familiar with another language or culture? Do you participate in a particular sport? Do you like to tinker with things? These pastimes—things we actually spend our free time on—can be a hidden resource.

Analyze Your Skills

Think of your skills in terms of the following categories:

- Interpersonal skills: warmth, sense of humor, empathy, cooperativeness, etc.
- Job skills: skills and technical knowledge related to a particular profession—accounting, plumbing, computer programming, etc.
- Transferable skills: skills that can be applied across disciplines (listed in the *Dictionary of Occupational Titles*).

The key to analyzing your skills is objectivity. Realistic self-assessment can be a little more difficult for people with disabilities because they often receive inappropriate feedback due to pity or prejudice. It seems that people either underestimate their abilities or overrate their accomplishments. Those who haven't had a chance to test themselves in a variety of employment situations don't have an objective standard of comparison to counterbalance these distortions.

Figure 4.1   Work Values Survey

I prefer these work factors
(check one box from each group that comes closest to your preference)

❏ Working for an organization ❏ Self-employment	❏ Working on a salaried or hourly basis ❏ Working on a commission or free-lance basis
❏ Full-time work ❏ Part-time work	❏ Working indoors ❏ Working outdoors
❏ Flexible hours ❏ Structured hours	❏ High responsibility ❏ Minimal responsibility
❏ Working alone ❏ Working with other people	❏ Motivated by money ❏ Motivated by personal satisfaction
❏ Fast pace ❏ Slow pace	❏ Close work with machines ❏ Little work with machines
❏ Working within a half-hour of home ❏ A long commute is okay	❏ Formal business environment ❏ Informal business environment
❏ Well-defined duties and responsibilities ❏ Room for creativity and initiative	❏ Work opportunities available after 65 ❏ Early retirement
❏ Close or moderate supervision ❏ Little or no supervision	❏ Many opportunities for advancement ❏ Advancement isn't important
❏ Working in a large, open space ❏ Working in a small, restricted area	❏ Guaranteed regular hours ❏ Possibility of overtime
❏ Work that offers security ❏ Work that is interesting, but may offer little security	❏ Working with people with disabilities ❏ Working with people without disabilities
❏ High prestige and status ❏ Prestige and status aren't important	❏ Working in a specific geographic area ❏ Willing to relocate
❏ Working in the city ❏ Working in the country	❏ Working with children or senior adults ❏ Working with adults
❏ Working with things ❏ Working with information	❏ Outside social activities available through job ❏ Social activities aren't important
❏ Need benefits package ❏ Benefits aren't important	❏ Working at a desk ❏ Being mobile in work

---

Figure 4.1 (*Continued*)

❑ Frequent travel	❑ Seeing tangible end products
❑ Little or no travel	❑ Dealing in long-range goals
❑ Being the boss	❑ Working with the less fortunate
❑ Being supervised by others	❑ Working with the mainstream population
❑ Working for a large company	❑ Bringing work home
❑ Working for a small company	❑ Leaving work at work
❑ Routine assignments	❑ Working in the private sector
❑ Variety in work	❑ Working for the government or a nonprofit agency
❑ Need to be on a public transportation line	❑ _____
❑ Public transportation isn't important	❑ _____

Source: Melanie Astaire Witt, *Job Strategies for People with Disabilities*. Princeton, N.J.: Peterson's, 1992, p. 51. Reprinted with permission. To order this book, write or call Peterson's, P.O. Box 2123, Princeton, NJ 08543-2123; 800/ 338-3282.

Inventory Your Experience

Your past is the key to your future. A powerful resume can open the door to many interviews. We will map out specific resume approaches in the next chapter. For now, step back and take stock of your experience—thoroughly, critically, and *in writing*. Using a job inventory sheet like the one in Figure 4.2, write down every position you've held. Include the title and a simple sentence describing each. My inventory began with a job scooping ice cream as a teenager.

Include Volunteer Work

Volunteer experience can be an important credential for jobseekers with disabilities because so many salaried positions have been closed to disabled workers. In reality, salaried jobs are only activities that are structured for the purpose of efficiency. This means that many of the skills you acquire through volunteer work could be transferable to a paid position. You might find that your responsibilities as president of the PTA match up very closely with the job description for a position as director of administration for a mid-sized company.

Finally, volunteer work reflects not only your marketable skills but also your commitment to being productive—even without pay.

After listing all your positions on the job inventory sheet, complete a job summary sheet for each one. Feel free to copy the sample form in Figure 4.3.

Figure 4.2 Job Inventory

Dates			
From	To	Job Title	Company
―――	―――	―――――――	―――――――
―――	―――	―――――――	―――――――
―――	―――	―――――――	―――――――
―――	―――	―――――――	―――――――
―――	―――	―――――――	―――――――
―――	―――	―――――――	―――――――
―――	―――	―――――――	―――――――
―――	―――	―――――――	―――――――
―――	―――	―――――――	―――――――
―――	―――	―――――――	―――――――
―――	―――	―――――――	―――――――
―――	―――	―――――――	―――――――

Number the positions chronologically, beginning with your earliest work and volunteer experiences. While part-time jobs in high school or college may not seem important, they reveal your emerging work ethic. If you worked to help your family with expenses, that shows a sense of responsibility.

Highlight Your Accomplishments

Notice that the job summary form allows more space for results than for responsibilities. That's because what you were supposed to do in a given position is far less important than what you actually did. Think carefully about how you solved problems, saved a company money, improved productivity, implemented new procedures, reduced waste, enhanced customer service, and so forth.

Also consider your accomplishments outside of work: Were you a top fund-raiser for your church or school alumni group? Did you organize any efforts to promote access for people with disabilities in your community— a traffic signal, ramp entry to a public building, or designated parking

Figure 4.3   Job Summary Sheet

Job No. _____

_____ to _____
   year   year

Company name _____ _____

Job title_____

Significant responsibilities (in order of importance)

1._____

2._____

3._____

Significant results (in order of importance)

1._____

2._____

3._____

4._____

5._____

spaces? Did you organize any support groups or training for people with disabilities? Did you learn to use a mouthstick for typing? Did you receive any high school or college honors? Scholarships?

The first time through, your lists may be incomplete. With time, you will bring it all into sharper focus. Keep your completed summaries in a notebook or binder and revise them as you remember details. This process will sensitize you to the kind of job you want.

Focus on Job Requirement Competencies

With a general idea of your work values, interests, and experience, you are ready to zero in on specific job demands. To get a realistic idea of what employers are looking for today, study job announcements in newspapers, trade journals, employment offices. Whenever possible, get copies of actual job descriptions so that you can begin matching your profile with actual jobs.

People with disabilities often find that they meet the education, licensing, and experience requirements of a position but are unable to perform all the duties outlined in a job description or employment ad. Although most employers don't intend to discriminate against applicants with disabilities, they often do so by the way they frame job demands. You must learn to distinguish legitimate job requirements from an employer's wish list.

ADA AND THE ESSENTIAL FUNCTIONS TEST

The ADA is designed to ensure that qualified individuals with disabilities are not excluded from employment on the basis of arbitrary job requirements. It forces employers to pinpoint what functions are at the heart of each job.

Under the ADA, a job description can specify only *what* functions have to be performed, not *how* they are to be done.

For example, a position on a loading dock might require that 50-pound boxes be *moved* from place to place, but is it necessary that they be *lifted*, or could they be transported in a pushcart?

In a job involving computers, the essential function is to access, input, and retrieve information from the computer. A job applicant—someone with a visual limitation, for instance—does *not* have to be able to use the keyboard or visually read the screen if adaptive equipment or software would allow alternative ways to control the computer. The real question here is whether the acquisition of the equipment would be a reasonable accommodation. (More on this key concept in Chapters 12 and 13.)

The ADA also stipulates that a worker has to be able to perform only those duties that are essential to the position. Some employers require all job applicants to hold a valid driver's license, whether or not driving is needed in a particular position. This requirement is illegal under the ADA.

There are a few general guidelines to follow in determining if an employer's requirements are really essential to a particular position.

• The amount of time spent on the job performing the function. Although there is no specific percentage requirement, a function that is rarely performed might not be considered essential.
• The consequences of not performing the function. Although a firefighter might not often have to carry people down a ladder, failure to perform this function when necessary could have serious consequences.
• The position exists to perform that function. For a position proofreading documents, the ability to proofread would be essential because it is the reason the position exists.
• The number of employees among whom the function can be distributed is limited. In a small company, it may be necessary for each employee to

perform several functions. In this situation, functions that might not be essential if there were a larger staff have become essential because the staff size is small in relation to the volume of work.

RESOURCES FOR FURTHER SELF-ASSESSMENT

Today the market is flooded with motivational and instructional career guidance materials in print, audiotape, and computer formats.

Two good publications on taped resources are *The Audio Cassette Finder*, published by the National Information Center for Educational Media in Washington, DC (202/362-3444); and the *Video Source Book*, published by Gale Research in Detroit (313/962-2242).

Many excellent career workbooks are on the market: John Holland's *The Self-Directed Search*, available in both print and software; *Creating Careers with Confidence* by Edward Colozzi, available in braille from National Braille Press in Boston; and Barry and Linda Gale's *Discover What You're Best At: The National Career Aptitude System and Career Directory*.

Some publishing houses, such as Ten Speed Press of Berkeley, California (publisher of *What Color Is Your Parachute?*), and some computer software publishers, such as Cambridge Career Products of Charleston, West Virginia, specialize in career-related materials.

Are you considering a career in the sciences? The Project on Science, Technology, and Disability of the American Association for the Advancement of Science has compiled a *Resource Directory of Scientists and Engineers with Disabilities*. Do you think you might be able to work with computers? National Braille Press publishes several books that list names and addresses of people using computers in various occupations. Similar resources might be available from other organizations.

SITUATION ANALYSES

Situation No. 1

Kevin M. is a recent business school graduate who applied for a job as a marketing representative. He is blind.

The employer liked Kevin's background but can hire equally qualified sighted applicants. There is some automobile travel required. The employee hired receives a company car and travel reimbursement.

Does Kevin have a legal right to the job? Can he compel the employer to provide a driver? Can he compel the employer to change his job duties to limit the travel?

Analysis.   Initially, Kevin should recognize that he has no legal right to the job just because of his disability. There is no ADA requirement to hire a candidate with a disability over an equally qualified nondisabled candidate.

The issue of driving has to be looked at from an essential functions point of view. If driving is integral to the job, as it often is in marketing and sales positions, and if there is no way to restructure the job to eliminate that requirement without fundamentally changing the nature of the position, the employer can stand his ground on this requirement.

Because a sighted applicant wouldn't require a driver, Kevin had better approach the employer with a more creative alternative than hiring a driver. Perhaps a two-person sales effort would work successfully. Maybe Kevin could pay for the driver. He might even suggest a higher expense account instead of the car so that he can use taxis.

Limitation of Kevin's travel would probably be at the discretion of the employer, again depending on how essential it is to the position. As an entry-level worker, perhaps Kevin should be more realistic in his first career choice. He will never drive a car.

Situation No. 2

Charles L. is an administrator in the distribution center of a retail supermarket chain. He has a recurring spasm in his lower back that is aggravated by lifting anything heavier than 15 pounds.

The company's job description for an administrator does not mention any lifting duties. Charles learned that this was required the first day he accepted a transfer to the job.

Is the employer obligated to transfer Charles back to his former job? Must it eliminate the lifting requirement from his duties?

Analysis. If it's available, Charles probably is entitled to a transfer back to his former job. If not, the employer should eliminate the lifting requirement.

The ADA does not require employers to establish or maintain job descriptions. However, the fact that the employer has one is persuasive evidence that lifting is not an "essential function" of the job.

The ADA considers reassignment a reasonable accommodation but recognizes that other factors may preclude that option. Among them is the availability of the former job, the availability of comparable jobs, and the transfer policy of the employer.

There is no requirement to pay Charles the same amount for a job that pays less.

Situation No. 3

Laura W. has dyslexia and generally does poorly on written tests. She is a highly qualified commercial real estate agent.

The major commercial brokers require written preemployment tests. Laura would like to have the test waived entirely on the basis of her experience. If not, she would like to have the test "handicapped" to put her on an equal footing with nondisabled applicants. She is even thinking of requesting an oral exam.

How should Laura approach the issue with employers? What is their obligation to waive or modify the test?

Analysis. Laura should draw upon her self-confidence as a real estate agent and immediately state, "I have dyslexia. As a result, I have difficulty taking written tests."

Almost any creative option would show good faith on the part of the employer. Waiving the test for Laura might result in her being hired even though she is not the most qualified applicant. A better choice would be to administer the test orally. Even allowing additional time to take the test could easily be justified as a reasonable accommodation because the questions would still be testing her knowledge.

Unlike an occupation that requires the ability to read constantly (like copy editing), a real estate agent can easily work around this impairment on the job. In extreme cases, a person with dyslexia might be accommodated with a reader.

CHAPTER FIVE

Resumes and Cover Letters: Your Paper Profile

Some career counselors advise trying to arrange an interview without a resume; but in my 25 years in the placement field, I have found that about 90 percent of all interviews occur in response to a resume accompanied by a well-written cover letter. This traditional approach still works best.

THE RESUME

The self-assessment and job inventory you worked on in the preceding chapter will lay the groundwork for your resume. If you already have a resume, pull it out and take a fresh look at it. In *Jeff Allen's Best: The Resume*, I presented 100 power resume strategies. Let's review some of those tips and see how they apply to job seekers with disabilities.

Select a Format—Chronological or Functional

A chronological resume lists the positions in the order in which they were held, beginning with the most recent. Short-term employment can be combined or omitted. This format is the most straightforward and the easiest to construct. It works well for those who want to highlight a steady work record or prestigious employers. The downside is that the inclusion of dates accentuates gaps in employment and can open the door to age discrimination. If your disability has interrupted your record of employment, this format might not work for you.

First-time job hunters, reentry workers, career changers, and people who do not have a continuous work record often get better results with a functional resume—one that generalizes your duties and highlights selected skills and accomplishments. This format allows you to translate skills gained through volunteer work or work at home into marketable job skills. The downside here is that the indirect style can make an employer suspicious of your past instead of merely curious.

Because both formats have their pros and cons, many job seekers use a combination approach. This type of resume combines the flexibility of the functional with the specifics of the chronological. It allows you to emphasize the experience that is most relevant to the type of position you want. In drafting a combination resume, however, you must pay close attention to the structure and time line. People read resumes looking for a sense of history, years of experience, and so forth.

Stick to Basics

No matter what format you use, your resume should contain five basic elements: identification (name, address, and daytime phone number), career summary, experience, education, and references (see Figures 5.1 and 5.2). Many resumes also include a section on professional or community affiliations, awards, or other activities.

Keep It Short

The objective of a resume is not to get a job but to get an interview. The resume is a preview, presenting only enough information to answer the employer's immediate question: Why should I interview this applicant? After all, would you buy a book you've already read? The real test in crafting a resume is selecting, editing, and grouping the details of your career in a way that makes the employer want to know more about you. Cut anything that doesn't point up what you can do for an employer.

Reveal Only What Employer Needs to Know

Jobseekers with disabilities often find themselves interweaving their medical and professional histories by way of explaining gaps in employment or reasons for changing jobs. *Keep your medical history out of your resume.* If your disability is revealed in the types of jobs you've held (e.g., proofreader for National Braille Press), that's fine. If it's not, don't feel that you have to mention it to "explain" job changes or employment gaps.

Start with Career Summary

At the top of your resume, right below your name, address, and phone number, present a concise summary of your major attributes. Example: Advertising manager with 10 years' in-house and agency experience. Strong

Figure 5.1   Chronological Resume

Daniel J. O'Keefe
25 Sunnyside Lane
Walnut Creek, California 94596
(415) 965-5418

Summary: Management Systems Analyst with 10-year successful track record in systems analysis, design, and programming for Fortune 500 client companies. Skillful problem solver with a strong foundation in computer sciences, electrical engineering, and mathematics.

Experience and Accomplishments

1985–present   *Manager, Systems Design*
                    The Berkeley Group, Oakland, California

Managed team of 20 programmers, systems designers, and computer engineers for management consulting firm with revenue of more than $10 million per year.

• Designed new systems, supervised installation and initial operation, including orientation and training of client personnel.
• Served as liaison with senior management of client firms to develop objectives, review constraints, and recommend appropriate systems design.

1980–85   *Systems Analyst*
                    Electronic Solutions Corporation, Irvine, California

Top programmer and systems design expert with this innovative software development company.

• Led the team developing Write-Right™, a new word-processing program with grammar and spelling check features that has met with great market success.
• Redesigned ESC's order entry and shipping program, which resulted in 50% reduction in order-to-ship time.

Education: M.S., Computer Sciences, University of California at Irvine
                    B.S.E.E., California Polytechnic Institute, minor in
                    mathematics
Honors: Graduated *summa cum laude*, Member *Phi Beta Kappa*
Publications: Master's Thesis: "Computer Programming for IBM
                    Mainframes: A Systems Approach" published by University
                    Press
Special Skills   IDMS/IDD
and Knowledge: MVS INTERNALS
                    VM PERFORMANCE TUNING
                    Fluent in Spanish
References: Provided on request, once mutual interest has been
                    established.

Source: Reprinted with permission from Jeffrey G. Allen, *Jeff Allen's Best: The Resume.* New York: John Wiley & Sons, 1990, p. 105.

Figure 5.2   Combination Resume

MARILYN MORALES

65 Tinning Street   San Francisco, CA 94107   (415) 545-3379

COMPUTER SYSTEMS ANALYST

Strong background of more than 10 years as programmer/analyst developing, testing and documenting software on minicomputers and mainframe computers

---

COMPUTER SKILLS

LANGUAGES &
OPERATING SYSTEMS: ASSEMBLER, BASIC, C, COBOL, FORTRAN, MS-DOS, PASCAL

HARDWARE: Apple, Compaq, DEC, Hewlett-Packard, IBM, PRIME

WORK HIGHLIGHTS

* *Redesigned computer system with minimal equipment cost, resulting in a faster, more efficient program with total processing output increased 500%*
* *Directed staff of 10 in the conversion of a manual inventory system to a computerized system*
* *Designed, programmed, tested and documented a report generating program that tracked distribution of more than 1 million parts*
* *Trained and cross-trained 75 employees on all phases of company's computer system*
* *Chosen as team leader because of strong oral and written communication skills*

EXPERIENCE

Concord Pharmaceuticals   San Francisco, CA
Senior systems analyst   1989 to Present
Systems analyst   1987 to 1989
Conduct programming and research projects for manufacturer of pharmaceuticals

Willis Computer Laboratories   San Francisco, CA
Programmer   1981 to 1987
Developed, debugged, and documented software for company's customer billing system ($16M manufacturer of hardware and software with 4 divisions and 300 employees)

Figure 5.2   (*Continued*)

EDUCATION
University of California, Berkeley
B.S. Computer Science   **1981**
Held part-time jobs and paid all college tuition and expenses

---

PROFESSIONAL AFFILIATIONS
Association of Computer Professionals
Officer (president, vice president and treasurer)
of local chapter   **1989 to Present**

Source: Melanie Astaire Witt, *Job Strategies for People with Disabilities*.
Princeton, N.J.: Peterson's, 1992, p. 161. Reprinted with permission. To order this
book, write or call Peterson's, P.O. Box 2123, Princeton, NJ 08543-2123; 800/
338-3282.

idea person with track record in media relations, special promotions, direct
mail, and point-of-purchase campaigns.

I don't believe in stating a career objective because it can foreclose
other options.

List Only More Recent Positions

Employers want to know how great you will perform tomorrow, not what
you did 15 years ago. In fact, few of them check references beyond the two
or three most recent employers.

So, if you're wondering how to handle that gap between your fifth and
fourth jobs back in 1958, just cut from the bottom. This will also give you
more room to elaborate on your recent accomplishments.

Begin Sentences with Strong Action Words

Keep the "I" out of your resume and lead with the action:
"*Developed* a series of ..."
"*Organized* a task force ..."
"*Led* a team of researchers ..."
"*Managed* a program to ..."
Here are some effective action words:

Accelerated	Analyzed	Arranged
Accomplished	Applied	Attained
Achieved	Appointed	Audited
Administered	Arbitrated	Averted

Budgeted
Built
Calculated
Certified
Charted
Communicated
Compiled
Completed
Composed
Conceived
Conducted
Concluded
Constructed
Consulted
Contracted
Controlled
Converted
Convinced
Counseled
Cut
Created
Decentralized
Decided
Delivered
Demonstrated
Designed
Detected
Determined
Developed
Devised
Diagnosed
Directed
Discovered
Dispensed
Drafted
Edited
Eliminated
Established
Evaluated
Executed
Expanded
Expedited
Facilitated

Forecasted
Formulated
Founded
Generated
Guided
Handled
Headed
Identified
Implemented
Improved
Increased
Influenced
Initiated
Innovated
Installed
Instituted
Instructed
Introduced
Invented
Judged
Justified
Launched
Led
Maintained
Managed
Marketed
Maximized
Measured
Mediated
Modernized
Monitored
Motivated
Negotiated
Obtained
Operated
Ordered
Organized
Oversaw
Packaged
Participated
Performed
Pioneered
Planned

Prepared
Presented
Processed
Procured
Produced
Programmed
Promoted
Projected
Publicized
Published
Purchased
Raised
Recommended
Recruited
Reduced
Referred
Regulated
Reorganized
Reported
Represented
Researched
Resolved
Responded
Restored
Revamped
Revitalized
Selected
Served
Set up
Simplified
Sold
Solved
Staffed
Standardized
Streamlined
Strengthened
Studied
Succeeded
Summarized
Supervised
Supported
Synthesized
Systematized

Taught	Translated	Uncovered
Tested	Traveled	Undertook
Traded	Trimmed	Unified
Trained	Tripled	Upgraded

Emphasize Results

Don't just say you were a salesperson in a certain territory; indicate that sales increased during your job tenure. Use measurable standards wherever possible. Not "Was an effective telemarketer," but "Exceeded annual sales objective by 10 percent."

List Education Last

A brief mention of educational credentials and schools attended—without dates—should be the last item on the page. College degrees are easy for an employer to verify—and many of them do—so if you didn't earn a degree don't say you did. Something like this works just as well:

University of Nevada—4 years of undergraduate study in business administration

Drake University School of Law—2 years

Do It Yourself

Writing your own resume is something you *must* do to prepare yourself for an effective job search. Resume services make everyone's background sound the same, package them the same, and even send them to the same employers. Only you can tell your own story the way it should be told.

Polish to Perfection

Behind every great author is an editor, even when the masterpiece is a resume. If you don't really know English usage, pay someone to copy edit or proofread your work, looking at punctuation, spelling, grammar, consistency, sentence structure, word choice, layout alignments, and so forth. Few things are more frustrating than finding a typo or a missing line after you've printed 50 copies of your resume.

Neatness Counts

Your resume is your calling card, so you want it to project an image of competence, not one of limitation. You don't need to use expensive textured paper stock, but your resume should be professional looking: neatly typed on quality paper with adequate margins and effective use of white space. No erasures, white-outs, or smudges. If necessary, hire a typing service.

Resume Don'ts

- Don't exaggerate or mislead.
- Don't state a salary.
- Don't include names of references; "References upon request" will suffice.
- Don't give a reason for leaving previous jobs.
- Don't include a photograph.
- Don't reveal your age, race, height, weight, or marital status.

COVER LETTERS UNCOVER INTERVIEWS

The cover letter customizes your resume by highlighting areas of your experience that relate directly to the target job. The perfect cover letter shows how your unique combination of character, skill, and experience makes you the perfect candidate for the job.

Like your resume, the cover letter must be brief—no more than a page, please. The more you write, the less likely you are to be read. If you're a good writer, the cover letter is a chance to shine, and you'll fill your one page easily. If you're not, you can keep it short, simple, and courteous.

Unlike the resume, though, the cover letter must be tailored to each situation. A canned cover letter will "can" your chances for an interview.

Target Cover Letter

Don't attach a cover letter to a resume that's going to a personnel department. For them, it's just one more piece of paper to shuffle. The only real way to score an interview is to aim at a target, so always get a name. Don't send cover letters to "To whom it may concern" or "Dear sirs." If you are applying directly or through contacts, call ahead for the name and title of the person who would supervise your work. Regrettably, if you are responding to a blind ad that gives only a box number, you have no choice but to write "Dear Employer."

Learn about Position before Writing

The more you know about a position in advance, the better your cover letter will be. A call to the personnel department with three or four cogent questions can get you all you need to know to tailor your cover letter.

Limit Body of Letter to Three Paragraphs

- The *introductory paragraph*, which mentions the position you are inquiring about and how you heard about it.

• The *value paragraph*, which describes your background and major attributes. It's the longest paragraph, but not more than five or six sentences. It should be sincere and persuasive.

• The *action paragraph* which asks the interviewer to read your enclosed resume and to either contact you for an interview or anticipate your call within a few days.

The cover letter in Figure 5.3 uses two value paragraphs. One of them illuminates on-the-job experiences that compensate for the applicant's lack of a college degree, which was not a prerequisite at the time he entered his field.

Formatting Guidelines

Follow these guidelines when formatting your cover letter:

• Make each letter an original and sign it in black ink. Electric typewriters and word processors and computers with letter-quality printers produce the best results.
• Use a block-letter format (see Figure 5.4).
• Keep the length to one page.
• Check the layout. Copy should be centered on the page, neither too high nor too low; margins should be consistent (about ½ to ¾ inch left and right).
• Proofread the letter.
• Include your phone number in the return address at the top of the letter.

Follow Up Each Letter

Your delivery will be sharper on follow-up calls if you keep copies of your letters on hand to refresh your memory. Also, you can often pick up or modify parts of existing letters in your subsequent job inquiries.

Time Arrival of Response

The bigger the ad, the greater the number of responses it usually generates. People are seldom hired from the first batches of resumes, so resist the temptation to apply first. It's not a placement race. Time your resume to arrive somewhere in the middle of the following week. Avoid a Friday arrival. Friday is a day for firing, not hiring. Your resume will sit unopened until the following week, by which time it could be buried on someone's desk.

Figure 5.3   Sample Cover Letter

15587 Russell Street
Greenville, South Carolina 29602

December 5, 19___

Abigail N. Hardesty
Director of Human Resources
Quality Furniture Manufacturers, Inc.
1500 Magnolia Boulevard
Charleston, South Carolina 29401

Re: Third Shift Production Manager Position

Dear Ms. Hardesty:

Your advertisement in the most recent edition of the <u>Sunday</u>
<u>Star Ledger</u> called for a seasoned production manager to
handle third-shift operations at your Durham, North Carolina, plant.

The enclosed resume reflects that I am well qualified for
the position, with over 25 years' furniture manufacturing
experience. After graduation from high school, I began as
an equipment operator and progressed through scheduling,
purchasing, and inventory control to my current position as
Production Manager of the first shift at Rosewood Furniture's Greenville plant. The challenge of managing
Quality's much larger operation in Durham ignited my interest.

The "minimum educational requirements" specified in your ad
were a Bachelor's Degree in business administration, manufacturing management, <u>or its equivalent</u>. When I began my
career in 1964, a college education was not a prerequisite
for rising through the manufacturing ranks. Through extension study and "on-the-job training," I have gained experience in all facets of the production environment. In fact,
it is probably equivalent to several college degrees.

Rotating shift schedules have hampered my ability to attend
all of the night classes for a degree, but I have managed
to accumulate 65 credits toward a Bachelor of Science in
Administration with a concentration in Manufacturing Management, and I intend to keep working until I've completed
it.

I'll telephone you within the next week to set a convenient
meeting date.

Very truly yours,

Thomas Y. Crowell

Source: Reprinted with permission from Jeffrey G. Allen, *Jeff Allen's Best: Get the Interview*. New York: John Wiley & Sons, 1990, p. 91.

Figure 5.4   Block Letter Format

(return address)	xxxxxxxxxxxxx
	xxxxxxxxxxxxx
(date)	xxxxxxxxxxxxx

xxxxxxxxxxxx   (address)
xxxxxxxxxxx
xxxxxxxxxxx

Re:xxxxxxxxxxxxxxxxxxxx

xxxxxxxxxxxxxxxxxxxxxxxxxxx   (salutation)

xxxxxxxxxxxxxxxxxxxxxxxxxxxxxxxxxxxxxxxxxxxxxxxxxxxxxxxxxxxxxx
xxxxxxxxxxxxxxxxxxxxxxxxxxxxxxxxxxxxxxxxxxxxxxxxxxxxxxxxxxxxxx
xxxxxxxxxxxxxxxxxxxxxxxxxxxxxxxxxxxxxxxxxxxxxxxxxxxxxxxxxxxxxx

xxxxxxxxxxxxxxxxxxxxxxxxxxxxxxxxxxxxxxxxxxxxxxxxxxxxxxxxxxxxxx
xxxxxxxxxxxxxxxxxxxxxxxxxxxxxxxxxxxxxxxxxxxxxxxxxxxxxxxxxxxxxx
xxxxxxxxxxxxxxxxxxxxxxxxxxxxxxxxxxxxxxxxxxxxxxxxxxxxxxxxxxxxxx
xxxxxxxxxxxxxxxxxxxxxxxxxxxxxxxxxxxxxxxxxxxxxxxxxxxxxxxxxxxxxx
xxxxxxxxxxxxxxxxxxxxxxxxxxxxxxxxxxxxxxxxxxxxxxxxxxxxxxxxxxxxxx

xxxxxxxxxxxxxxxxxxxxxxxxxxxxxxxxxxxxxxxxxxxxxxxxxxxxxxxxxxxxxx
xxxxxxxxxxxxxxxxxxxxxxxxxxxxxxxxxxxxxxxxxxxxxxxxxxxxxxxxxxxxxx
xxxxxxxxxxxxxxxxxxxxxxxxxxxxxxxxxxxxxxxxxxxxxxxxxxxxxxxxxxxxxx
xxxxxxxxxxxxxxxxxxxxxxxxxxxxxxxxxxxxxxxxxxxxxxxxxxxxxxxxxxxxxx

xxxxxxxxxxxxxxxxxxxxxxxxxxxxxxxxxxxxxxxxxxxxxxxxxxxxxxxxxxxxxx
xxxxxxxxxxxxxxxxxxxxxxxxxxxxxxxxxxxxxxxxxxxxxxxxxxxxxxxxxxxxxx

(complimentary close)	xxxxxxxxxxxxxxx
(signature)	xxxxxxxxxxxxxxx

Call within Two Days

If you're sending out 15 or 20 cover letters, don't schedule them all to arrive on the same day because you may not be able to complete all the follow-up calls within the next week. You don't want your name to have faded from memory by the time you call.

The best times to call are between 9:00 A.M. and 10:00 A.M., before the day's meetings start, or after 4:00 P.M., when things have slowed down. If you don't get through the first time, try again. If you do, talk to the decision maker and ask for an interview. Your initial call might go something like this:

THEM: Human Resources, Emma Waverly.
YOU: Good morning, Ms. Waverly. This is William Tucker. I sent you a resume last week for the position of _____, and I'm calling to verify that you received it.
THEM: Just a moment. Let me check. Yes, it's here. It's being reviewed by our professional development staff at this time.
YOU: I have to decide on an offer soon, and I'd really like to talk to someone at Amalgamated before deciding. Can you tell me who's reviewing the resumes so that I can call and find out if I will be interviewed in the near future?
THEM: All right, Mr. Tucker. That would be Jim Farrell, extension 2345. He's the department manager.
YOU: Thank you, Ms. Waverly.

It might not go so well in every instance. Your request could be met with a "don't call us, we'll call you" response. In that case, thank the person and say good-bye. If you push too hard, your resume could land in the wastebasket in retaliation.

SITUATION ANALYSES

Situation No. 1

Vincent T. has one arm. He wants to apply for work as a dental assistant. His resume has a line that says "Health: Excellent." When a dental clinic calls him for an interview, he becomes concerned that the health statement on his resume will lose his protection under the ADA.

At the interview, he notices that most of the equipment can be easily adapted to someone with one arm.

Has Vincent misrepresented his health? Can he be denied employment for not disclosing his disability? Must the clinic allow him to show that he can use the equipment successfully?

Analysis. Vincent is wasting a good worry.

Aside from his stress, his health *is* excellent for a dental assistant's job. Even if he had several disabilities, the only issue is whether they are "job-related functional limitations."

Because using the equipment is an essential function of the position, it would appear reasonable under the circumstances for the employer to ask how Vincent would use it. His willingness to demonstrate would work in his favor.

Many employers panic and ease disabled applicants out the door with some variation of "Don't call us, we'll call you." The unspoken words that follow are "... and please don't report us to the authorities." Too many disabled applicants believe they'll never be hired anyway, so they don't bother to discuss alternatives.

But Vincent? A little persistence should have him on the job Monday morning.

Situation No. 2

Frank V. is a paraplegic commercial photographer. He wants to cold call photography studios in the metropolitan Yellow Pages to screen them before wheeling in for an interview. He would like employers to get to know him before he mentions his disability. His portfolio of past projects is excellent.

Is Frank legally waiving his rights under the ADA by not mentioning his access requirements? If the studio doesn't have wheelchair access when he arrives, can he demand to be interviewed outside? If he is then qualified, can he demand to have the necessary workplace alterations made to accommodate his chair? How can he find out whether the studio is responsible as a "covered entity" under the ADA?

Analysis. Frank hasn't waived any rights by not disclosing his disability, but he may not have any rights to waive.

"Covered entities" are those businesses that presently have 25 or more employees (including part-timers) working for 20 or more calendar weeks. This number will be reduced to 15 in July 1994.

Frank should call to find out how many employees each studio has. If it is under the ADA minimum, the employer is exempt from federal regulation. The next call should be to the appropriate state agency. If the state has a lower requirement, that will apply.

Even if a studio is a covered entity, Frank can't insist on an interview outside. Changing the workplace to accommodate wheelchair access is often a complicated process involving landlords, tenants, attorneys, contractors, and government officials. Frank would be best advised to file a charge of discrimination with the EEOC or state agency, then go on to the next interview.

Situation No. 3

Yvonne M. is applying for a data entry position. She states on her resume: "If I am hired, I will require a height-adjustable chair with full back support and arm rests." Actually, she will need far more, since she is paralyzed on her left side.

Yvonne was advised to do this by a resume service. The manager reasoned that employers who would screen her out because of the chair requirement would not be receptive to more accommodations.

Yvonne is sensitive about her disability and fears rejection.

Should she change the words on her resume? If so, what should she write? Would it help to mention her requirements in a cover letter instead of on the resume?

Analysis. Yvonne should do more than change the words on her resume— she should eliminate them.

A resume is a direct-mail piece. It will get anywhere from 0 to 45 seconds of attention on the initial screening. Yvonne's resume might as well be a red octagon with white letters that spells, "Stop!"

While some authorities recommend mentioning any needed accommodations in a cover letter, this authority doesn't. This authority has never seen a single person get hired by mentioning a disability at that fragile, impersonal, prescreening stage. This authority wants you to get hired, not tired.

It's not the disability that stops most jobseekers with disabilities. It's the failure to market themselves properly.

CHAPTER SIX

Job
Leads

Job hunting is a full-time job. That means studying the market, making phone calls, sending out resumes, and talking to contacts every day. Your chances of finding a job increase with every lead you pursue.

RESEARCH

Search Your Target

If you're aiming at a particular company, call and request a brochure or catalog that will tell you about its programs, corporate policies, and products. If it's a public company, you can ask for a copy of its annual report.

As a jobseeker with disabilities, you want to pay particular attention to the company's affirmative action profile, track record in hiring people with disabilities, and commitment to worker training. An indispensable source for this kind of information is *CAREERS & the disABLED*, a periodical published by Equal Opportunity Publications (150 Motor Parkway, Greenlawn, NY 11788-5145; 516/273-0066). Each issue contains an affirmative action career directory of employers committed to recruiting people with disabilities. The magazine also offers a resume service. Jobseekers can send their resumes to the magazine to be forwarded to specified employers.

If you are trying to compile a list of companies for consideration, consult any of the following sources in your public library:

Directory of Corporate Affiliations
Directory of Executive Recruiters

Dun & Bradstreet's Million-Dollar Directory
Forbes: Annual Report of American Business
Forbes 500
Fortune 500
Hoover's Handbook: Profiles of over 500 Major Corporations
MacRae's Blue Book
Moody's Manuals
Moody's News Reports
Standard Directory of Advertisers
Standard & Poor's Register of Corporations, Directors, and Executives
Thomas's Register of American Manufacturers
U.S. Industrial Product Directory
Value Line Investment Surveys
Wall Street Journal Index
100 Best Companies to Work for in America

Just be sure you don't spend all your time *researching* instead of *searching*. Many of these references are designed for investors, so you might have to read between the lines to glean the information you need.

Use the Telephone

Sales, marketing, customer service, public relations, and personnel departments are good sources of information. These are staff functions accustomed to telephone inquiries. Receptionists and secretaries can be very helpful if you establish rapport with them. If they don't have the answers to your questions, they will readily route you to someone who does.

Here are some questions you can ask to obtain general company information:

- How long has the business been in operation?
- How many people does it employ?
- Where is it headquartered?
- What divisions does the company have?
- What are the business's annual sales?
- What are the business's main products or services?
- What markets does the business serve?
- Does the company employ an EEO officer or a disabilities coordinator?

Instead of asking direct questions about job *openings*, make general inquiries about job *opportunities* and the nature of the company. If your information call becomes a job-hunting call, you will be transferred to the human resources department, where you'll get the standard line: "Send a resume and we'll review it."

Read Classified Ads

Only about 15 percent of available jobs are advertised in newspaper classifieds, but this is still a good place to start. Even if you're not relocating, don't limit yourself to local papers. There are several national job listings that appear weekly, the best of which is the *National Business Employment Weekly* (420 Lexington Avenue, New York, NY 10170; 212/808-6796). It's a compilation of all the job listings that appeared in *The Wall Street Journal* that week. If you're looking for a job in the federal government, consult the *Federal Jobs Digest*. Some publications contain nothing but job ads: the *National Weekly Job Report, Affirmative Action Register, Physical Therapy/ Occupational Therapy Job News.*

Make Job Research a Habit

Gathering intelligence on target employers is easier if you do it regularly. Read trade magazines, national business publications such as *Fortune* and *Forbes*, and the business section in your local newspaper for information on mergers, buyouts, and downsizes. Find out what companies are hiring, which are laying off, who's relocating into or out of your area, etc.

Don't regard the job search as something you do until you find a new job. Keep an eye on your career horizon and you'll never be blown away when the winds shift.

Move Up instead of Out

As I told millions of career catatonics in *Surviving Corporate Downsizing*, every company—even the one you're working for—is a mini-job market. In one sense, marketing yourself to your current employer is easier than breaking into a new company. You know the idiosyncrasies of supervisors, the coworkers who sleepwalk through the day, and the jobs that never get done. You also know the corporate culture—its commitment to equal employment opportunity, its attitudes towards workers with disabilities, its flexibility in accommodating workers' needs. In marketing terms, you know the audience.

Networking

Networking became a career guidance buzzword in the 1970s. Formal and informal career networks sprang up everywhere, and pretty soon networking was getting in the way of working. This strategy has fallen out of favor with some career experts, but in my experience it is still the secret success weapon in every superstar's arsenal. It is a *net* to keep you *working*. The U.S. Department of Labor's statistics indicate that 80 percent of people who find jobs in this country do so by networking.

Use Personal and Professional Contacts

Make a comprehensive list of everyone you know—from your best friend to your barber. That includes former coworkers and supervisors, former professors or deans, directors of volunteer organizations, politicians, ministers or rabbis, etc. Then cast your net to find out what they know about companies that are hiring. Ask if they know of an employer with a position open in your line of work. Also ask if they would be willing to call and make an introduction for you or if you can use their name when you call. Be grateful for what they can do and don't resent what they can't.

Your accountant, lawyer, stockbroker, insurance agent, financial planner—anyone whose services you've purchased—can be a great resource. One of their clients could become your next employer.

The following dialogue represents the actual experience of one job seeker who went from an anonymous midlevel job in a large company to a successful top management post at a smaller firm. The job wasn't advertised—he found it by picking up the phone and calling his accountant.

RECEPTIONIST: Good morning. Brophy & Associates, Certified Public Accountants.

MARK: Good morning. I'd like to speak to Dean Brophy, please. This is Mark Gibson calling.

DEAN: Mark! I didn't expect to hear from you until tax season. Is there something I can do for you?

MARK: As a matter of fact there is. When we got together earlier this year, I told you I went back to school to complete my MBA. My job as an engineer had stalled and I was trying to give my career a boost.

DEAN: I remember. How's it going?

MARK: Well, I'm about ready to graduate and I'm organizing my job search. When we talked, you mentioned that a client—a small steel company—needed some reorganization. Do you think they could use a structural engineer with an MBA to help streamline them? My concentration is in finance, and I have a lot of steel experience.

DEAN: I'm glad you called. We're just about to pull together a new management team for the company, and your qualifications might be just what we need. Why don't we get together and talk this week, and then we'll arrange to meet with the client. Can you be here Thursday at 4:00?

MARK: I'll be there. And I'll stop by today and drop off my resume for you to review in the meantime.

DEAN: Good enough. Goodbye, Mark, and thanks for calling.

More on how to use contacts to open doors in Chapter 7.

Find a Mentor

A mentor is a combination father, mother, teacher, public relations person, coach, and guide—someone who believes in your potential and wants to advance your career. A mentor is usually someone in senior management; however, you might find it helpful to have a mentor who has a disability and can show you the ropes of the company from that point of view.

Join Professional or Trade Associations

Professional and trade groups are an invaluable networking medium. Their meetings, conferences, and trade shows give you a forum to make face-to-face contacts while learning about the issues and trends in a profession. Many associations tape their seminars and conferences and make them available for a modest price. Some associations offer career placement services or have informal employment committees to help members find jobs; others publish job opportunities in their newsletters. Membership directories can be used for one-on-one networking.

The *Encyclopedia of Associations,* published by Gale Research and available in major libraries, lists organizations dedicated to virtually every business pursuit. Most associations are structured around local chapters. Some even have subgroups organized around the issue of disability. The American Psychological Association, for instance, has an active disabled membership.

Contact Disability-Specific Associations

In addition to trade and professional associations, there are literally hundreds of associations for people with disabilities. Some, such as the Arthritis Foundation or the National Center on Employment of the Deaf, offer job placement services, vocational rehabilitation, career counseling, and assistive technology. Organizations such as the American Council of the Blind serve as umbrellas to many special interest groups such as blind educators, lawyers, computer specialists, and so forth.

The appendix to this book lists some of the major self-help organizations for people with disabilities.

Join—or Form—a Job Club

Job clubs can help you get a feel for the local employment market and give you emotional support at little or no cost. Formal groups are sponsored by a local government agency, college, or community organization. Meetings are led by qualified job counselors. Informal clubs are sponsored by a group of unemployed people. A job club, usually composed of 15 or 20 people, keeps you motivated and gives you the support you need during the job-hunting process. Informal clubs are usually run by members, but they often invite headhunters and personnel directors to speak at meetings.

Along these same lines, if you already own a piece of adaptive equipment such as a paperless braille device, you could join a user's group as a way of networking.

PLACEMENT SERVICES—PUBLIC AND PRIVATE

Consult the appendix for a more detailed listing of government-sponsored and private employment services for people with disabilities.

State Vocational Rehabilitation Agencies

These agencies offer people with disabilities an array of job-related assistance, ranging from job counseling and training to placement and referral. Agencies may fund all or partial costs of needed training, assistive technology, or other accommodations for eligible individuals.

If you choose to use these services, don't relinquish control of your career to your counselor. Rami Rabby and Diane Croft, authors of *Take Charge: A Strategic Guide for Blind Job Seekers*, published by National Braille Press, recommend that you know what kind of work you want to do and what skills you have to offer before you make an appointment. If you don't, the rehab counselor will take charge. He or she will enroll you in a training program, select your adaptive equipment, and even choose your employer. You will have a job, but you will have learned very little about the job-hunting process.

U.S. Employment Service

Through more than 1,700 state and local offices nationwide, this agency provides jobseekers with disabilities a wide range of services, including employability assessments, job counseling, training referrals, job placement, and trained specialists to work with job seekers. It circulates information about local, state, and national job openings and training opportunities as well as occupational demand and supply information with particular labor markets.

Independent Living Centers

About 400 independent living centers around the country provide vocational and employment services, adaptive aid loans, recruitment services, job training, referral to specialized technical assistance resources, and other services to enable individuals with severe disabilities to function independently.

Committees on Employment of People with Disabilities

The President's Committee on Employment of People with Disabilities works with state organizations, governors' and mayors' committees, and disability rights advocacy organizations (called President's Committee Partners) to increase employment opportunities for people with disabilities. President's Committee Partners provide technical assistance on employment and workplace accommodations.

Projects with Industry

More than 125 federally funded local projects involving small and large businesses, trade associations, foundations, community agencies, and the rehabilitation community create and expand job and training opportunities for individuals with disabilities. Contact the International Association of Business, Industry, and Rehabilitation for information on local projects (PO Box 15242, Washington, DC 20003; 202/543-6353).

Public Employment Offices

Don't overlook your state employment office (sometimes called the "unemployment" office), which offers free assistance to all jobseekers. People with disabilities are guaranteed service by law, although budget cuts have eliminated the requirement for disability-specific counselors. Keep in mind that this is a huge bureaucracy—impersonal, inefficient, and overburdened. Many people view it as a court of last resort.

Executive Recruiters

Known in the industry as "headhunters," executive search firms are the exclusive agents of employers. They are hired to find candidates with established track records to fill midlevel and senior management positions paying $50,000 and up. Executive recruiters find desirable job candidates, interview them, and check their references. They prepare written reports on finalist candidates for review by client employers. Executive recruiters are generally more interested if they find you first. That usually involves having your name given to them by someone else.

A growing number of executive search firms are specializing in certain occupations, industries, or geographic areas.

Employment Agencies

If your search is in the $30,000 annual salary range, executive recruiters won't even talk to you—but employment agencies will. In recent years, most agencies have changed their fee policies from applicant-paid to employer-paid. That means they are working for the employer, not the job seeker. Their goal is to find people for jobs, not jobs for people.

College Placement Offices

Even if you graduated from college 20 years ago, call your alma mater's placement office and see what services they offer. In addition to job listings, many offer their alumni skills testing, resume-writing assistance, and other services at no charge.

Temporary Agencies

Temporary agencies are one of the fastest growing industries in the United States, providing work not just for those between jobs but also for thousands of qualified people who cannot work full time. Temporary work is a good way to explore nontraditional opportunities without having to make a lifelong commitment. Although placement of office support staff and factory workers represents the bulk of temporary agencies' business, their range is widening to include the professional temporary: computer programmers, data processors, librarians, and even doctors, nurses, and lawyers. Recent studies by the National Association of Temporary Services show that 54 percent of temps are subsequently hired to stay on the job full time.

Temporary work can be a way for a disabled job seeker to prove what he or she can do. However, an employer in this context is likely to be reluctant to invest in an accommodation.

TELEPHONE TECHNIQUES

A cold call telemarketing effort can yield results if you have good verbal skills and self-confidence. Although it's easier to be misinterpreted on the telephone than in person, you won't be prejudged on physical appearance or style of dress.

Use the research sources mentioned earlier in this chapter to compile your cold call list of employers.

Target Your Call

Your two most likely targets in a cold-calling campaign would be someone in human resources or a department manager. Human resources people screen applicants and arrange interviews. Department managers make the actual hiring decisions.

In her book *Job Strategies for People with Disabilities*, Melanie Witt recommends a simple two-call approach to find out a department manager's name. First call and tell the switchboard operator you are sending correspondence to the manager and need the correct name spelling and title. A day or two later, call back and ask for that person directly, making no mention of your first call.

Plan Your Script

I'm not suggesting by any means that you prepare a "canned" approach—that will get you nowhere. You do, however, have to have some idea of what you will say when the phone is picked up.

- Are you going to ask for a job up front?
- Are you going to say anything about your disability?
- How will you get past the gatekeeper to speak to the decision maker?

Consider this conversation initiated by a computer professional with a visual impairment.

SECRETARY: Good morning. Information systems department.
JOB SEEKER: Good morning, my name is George Akins. I'm calling for Ms. Cooper.
SECRETARY: I'm sorry but she's in a meeting right now. May I ask what this is in regard to?
JOB SEEKER: I am a skilled database manager who is covered by the Americans with Disabilities Act due to a visual impairment. I'm not looking for a job at your company, but I would like to talk to Ms. Cooper about targeting my search. I need just a few minutes of her time to get some advice and possibly a referral.
SECRETARY: Why don't you send her a resume and cover letter so she can get back to you.
JOB SEEKER: I'll do that. But if her schedule permits, I would appreciate your help in setting up an interview so I can talk to her in person as well. What time do you expect her back from the meeting?
SECRETARY: It should be over around noon.
JOB SEEKER: In that case I'll try to reach her then. In the meantime, will you

let her know that I called for an information interview at her earliest convenience? And thanks for your help.

Perfect Your Delivery

Do you really know how you come across on the phone? Does your voice sound professional, assertive, persuasive? If you don't know, find out. Before you talk to a job lead, pick up the handset and talk to yourself.

You can use your answering machine for this. Prepare a script, then call yourself up and record your conversation. It's helpful to have a friend waiting for your call to act as an interviewer. Either way, be sure the call is recorded on your machine. Play it back and evaluate both content and delivery: Are you enunciating clearly, or are you slurring your words together? Do you have any noticeable verbal tics such as "you know," "um," and "like"? Are you talking too fast? Too slow? Are you speaking in a monotone?

Practice, record, listen, then practice again until your telephone delivery is effective.

Attach Mirror to Telephone

A smile on your face puts a smile in your voice. If you're slumped over the phone in your bathrobe with a glum look on your face, that image will be reflected in your voice. Get dressed, straighten up, and smile. When you see that polished professional smiling back at you from the mirror, your self-assurance will be conveyed over the phone.

Importance of Timing

Statistically, the best time to reach an interviewer in the personnel department is Tuesday through Friday between 9:00 A.M. and 11:00 A.M. Mondays are unpredictable and should be avoided. There's probably a deluge of calls from weekend ads, Friday's backlog of paperwork, and new hires to process.

Friday mornings are generally a good time because that's when most employees who are quitting give notice. The personnel department might learn of an opening on a Friday and agree to schedule an interview for you the following week.

Tuesday through Friday mornings are also good times to reach departmental decision makers.

Avoid Rejection Shock

Job hunting can be a "no" business, so you have to avoid rejection shock. If you get a "no interest" response to your best interview delivery, don't immediately dial the next number on your list. Take time out to regain your perspective so that you won't carry over any negativity or resentment into the next call. Each call is a new beginning; but if you contract rejection shock, each call will become a self-fulfilling prophecy—rejection. Keep reminding yourself that there are some 100 million jobs out there—and you only need one of them.

SITUATION ANALYSES

Situation No. 1

Trudy P. was contacted at her job as a corporate controller by an independent executive recruiter. She tells the recruiter that she has a history of ovarian cancer but believes she can pass a routine physical examination. He says he will have to reveal the condition to clients when he presents her background.

A job opportunity has arisen through the recruiter, and Trudy really wants to interview for it. Can she legally prevent the recruiter from mentioning the disability by citing the ADA? Is her constitutional right to privacy being violated? Does the recruiter have any responsibility as a "covered entity" under the ADA?

Analysis. The ADA has no provision that enables Trudy to stop the recruiter from mentioning her history of ovarian cancer. However, federal and state equal employment opportunity laws protect jobseekers from discrimination based on "medical condition." This is the area where the recruiter is vulnerable.

Trudy's constitutional right to privacy may also be violated, but the Equal Employment Opportunity Commission (EEOC) has no jurisdiction to enforce that right. She would probably have to bring a lawsuit in her local U.S. district court.

The recruiter is clearly a covered entity (even if he has no employees) because he is considered an "employment agency" under all equal employment opportunity laws, including the ADA.

Situation No. 2

Walter A. lost the use of both legs while serving in the army, but he is adept at using crutches and can maneuver without difficulty.

He reads about a job fair at a private convention center. The facility has donated its space to a group of local businesses because unemployment in the area is high. All the participating employers fully comply with the ADA in their hiring decisions. The facility has no ramps, handrails, or other accommodations for people with disabilities, but it is the only feasible place in the area to hold this type of event.

Can the ADA prevent the job fair from being held? Does Walter have the right to file a charge of discrimination with the EEOC? Can the facility owners successfully argue that it would be an "undue hardship" to alter a donated facility? Can they obtain a formal exemption from the EEOC?

Analysis. The EEOC can have the job fair enjoined (stopped) in U.S. district court because it is in direct violation of the ADA. The convention facility is clearly a "place of public accommodation."

Walter himself doesn't have standing to file a charge of discrimination because he is not being directly injured; he is able to enter the premises. However, he can report the violation and the EEOC will enforce the law.

There is no "undue hardship" defense for a voluntary contributor. But the ADA is not designed to prevent community activities that incidentally discriminate against the disabled while also giving them an opportunity.

The EEOC will look favorably on any "mitigation" of the problem, such as holding a portion of the fair outdoors if possible.

Situation No. 3

Donna P. is a former drug addict with highly specialized experience in genetic engineering. She said nothing about her drug history to a pharmaceutical company that offered her the best job of her life.

Today Donna received a confirming letter along with an eight-page document entitled "Habitual Drug User Questionnaire." The questionnaire is to be completed and returned immediately. She had no idea it existed, and it was never mentioned in her interviews. Friends in the know have warned her that the offer will be revoked if she admits to a history of drug abuse.

Must Donna answer the questionnaire? Does she have to confess to her prior drug abuse? Should she contact the EEOC and file a charge of discrimination? Will that protect her job?

Analysis. Donna is protected against discrimination in employment based on her former drug addiction. Even someone enrolled in a drug rehabilitation program is protected.

I wouldn't advise her to falsify the answers to the questionnaire. This employer's perceived "business necessity" can't justify discriminating against someone with a history of drug addiction.

Donna (or her lawyer) should call the person who sent the questionnaire and tell him or her that it will be answered. Then the start date should be confirmed because Donna will definitely be reporting for work.

No rational hiring authority would dare to mention the questionnaire again.

Situation No. 4

Teri M. has a severe speech impediment caused by emotional trauma when she was a child. She applies for a position as a technical systems analyst that requires limited verbal communication. However, she is concerned that her speech impediment will interfere with her interviewing.

What should she do?

Analysis. Teri needs to think strategically.

Even though her speech impediment is a psychological condition, she is considered disabled. The ADA prohibits employers from disqualifying people with disabilities that affect only marginal or nonessential job functions.

But employers have their ways of screening people, and Teri may be carefully rejected with no proof of discrimination. If she knows a technical recruiter, she should ask for assistance. Even though recruiters are paid by employers, most can enter into this kind of arrangement with a job seeker without a state "applicant-pays-fee" license.

For a nominal fee, the recruiter can make the presentation by phone, arrange the interview, and do the necessary follow-up for Teri. That's the problem, though—employers are less likely to work with these agencies. Many prefer candidates who make the initial contact themselves as a sign of self-sufficiency. Right or wrong, Teri had better know the rules.

Recruiters are professionals at placing. A good one will have Teri off the street and in front of the computer screen fast.

CHAPTER SEVEN

Positioning
Your References
for Maximum Impact

Entertainers have agents. Jobseekers have references. References are one of the most underestimated job-hunting resources. Most people fall back on only two predictable sources—former supervisors and instructors. But jobseekers with physical challenges can't afford to overlook references. *You* might know that you can do the job, but a skeptical employer will want to hear it from someone who has actually seen you in action—both on and off the job. Whether or not you have a disability, what someone else says about you has more impact and credibility than what you say about yourself.

The key to turning lackluster references into supercharged testimonials is positioning. In this chapter we'll look at ways to position your references for maximum impact. The suggestions here are adapted from my book *The Perfect Job Reference.*

WHEN TO USE THEM

The first element of positioning is knowing when to use your references. They can be used effectively at both the preinterview and postinterview stages in your job hunt. As I mentioned in Chapter 5, you don't want to list them on the resume because that relinquishes your control over who is contacted and when. Think strategically about how to deploy your supporters. Depending upon the circumstances and the personality of the individual, you can:

- Have references call on your behalf before you send in a resume.
- Send a reference cover letter along with your resume when making an initial job inquiry (see Figure 7.1).
- Use references to strengthen your candidacy with a letter or phone call after the interview (see Figure 7.2).

HOW TO CHOOSE THEM

A second element in positioning is selection. The bottom line is that you want people who know you, like you, and want to help you succeed.

Don't get into a reference rut by using the same few people for every position. Choose your references for impact. If one job requires the ability to supervise, draw upon people who can attest to your management skills. If another job requires analytical skills, revive the staff accountant from your last job. The idea is to match the people with the job.

The process of lining up your references is the same process you used in culling your contacts. Take a careful look back at your work history, dig out those business cards from people you've met along the way, and compile a list of names and phone numbers. Here, too, the people will fall into two broad categories—professional and personal.

Professional References

Work-related references are generally more potent than academic ones because businesses want tangible services. Your list of professional references should include:

- Your supervisors—present and former.
- Your boss's boss and other top executives who have seen your work at your present or former place of employment.
- Coworkers—past and present.
- Subordinates who can testify to your management ability.
- Members of trade and professional associations.
- Vocational counselors.
- Managers of support departments who worked with you.
- Key employees of consulting firms and other vendors whose services you used.
- Key employees of client firms.

From this list of possibilities, try to lock up at least six professional references suitable for framing.

Figure 7.1 Sample Preinterview Reference Letter

American Foods Company
2204 Mercantile Building
Chicago, Illinois 60626
(312) 974-0700

Angela P. Edwards, Director
Market Research

April 3, 19__

Margaret O. Blaine, Product Manager
Convenience Foods Division
American Foods Company
1667 Commonwealth Avenue
Boston, MA 02210

Re: Amanda F. Harston Reference

Dear Marge:

I hope all is going well with your new product launch. Last November, when my department gave you that revised market research you needed, you asked me to let you know if you could return the favor. Well, now you can.

My associate and friend, Amanda Harston, is applying for the assistant product manager position that opened at the breakfast division of American. In addition to great credentials, Amanda has the energy, insight, and dedication needed to be an outstanding assistant product manager.

As the enclosed resume shows, Amanda recently enhanced her ten years' experience in product marketing at XYZ, Inc., with an MBA from Bentley College. She graduated with high honors in spite of a 60-hour-a-week job that required 70 percent travel time. Although she has moved up steadily at XYZ, now that she has solid experience and graduate credentials, she'd like a larger environment.

I'm hoping that you will ask John Lawson, who is hiring for this position, to take the time to interview Amanda. Once he meets her, he will probably feel he owes you a favor.

If you'd like to know more about Amanda before you present her credentials to John, give me a call.

Best regards,

Angela P. Edwards

Source: Adapted from Jeffrey G. Allen, *The Perfect Follow-up Method to Get the Job.* New York: John Wiley & Sons, 1992, p. 116. Reprinted with permission.

Figure 7.2   Sample Postinterview Reference Letter

Employers Insurance Companies
Corporate Headquarters
One Pioneer Plaza
Chicago, Illinois 60610
(312) 555-0100

March 18, 19__

James Page
Chief Financial Officer
General Investors Group
1200 Park Avenue
New York, New York 10011

Re: Sam Abrams Reference

Dear Mr. Page:

As chief financial officers of multinational companies, you and I know how important the internal audit process is to our financial stability. But talented audit managers are hard to find.

My associate, Sam Abrams, is one of them. A 15-year veteran of multinational audit management, Mr. Abrams used his keen understanding of the audit process to develop solutions to complex financial problems.

Mr. Abrams reported directly to me in my former position as CFO at Amalgamated Industries. Now that you've had the opportunity to speak with him, I'm sure you can see how much you could benefit from his expertise and his outstanding record of training at Wharton. His use of a wheelchair in no way impinges upon his skills, productivity, availability, or enthusiasm.

If you would like any further information about Mr. Abrams, don't hesitate to call.

Sincerely,

Benjamin Rothe

Personal References

Employers used to disregard personal references as people who had a vested interest in the applicant's success—who either depended on the person for support or who were owed money. But times have changed. With all the constraints on what companies can say about their former employees, personal references are becoming a more credible source of information about a job applicant's character and experience.

Take out a sheet of paper and list 50 friends, acquaintances, neighbors, community leaders, and others you see socially outside of work. Include everyone from your current best friend to casual acquaintances. Then add business advisors such as your attorney, accountant, or bankers. You're looking for three characteristics:

- A strong professional reputation
- A self-confident, outgoing demeanor
- Good communications skills

You can even get references from people who don't know you that well. If you're the type of person who takes the time to talk with a banker after closing a loan, who invites the school principal out for coffee after a PTA meeting, or who volunteers for civic activities, your list will probably have far more than 50 names. From that initial list of 50 you're going to screen and sort to arrive at your top 5 personal references.

HOW TO PREPARE THEM

The final element in positioning is preparation. If you want your references to pull rabbits out of a hat, you have to put them there. Try this three-step process for activating your supporters.

Step 1: Enlist Their Support

No matter how well you know a person, you have to follow protocol when using him or her as a reference. That means getting permission to use their name. This is best done in a brief phone call. Here's an example from *The Perfect Job Reference.*

JOB SEEKER: Joe, good to hear your voice again. It's Vince Bailey. Did you get that article I sent last month on semiconductor research?

I have another reason for calling today. I'll only keep you a minute. I've decided it's time to move on. The reorganization here has limited the opportunity for advancement, so I've decided to look around for a director position. This is confidential, of course.

Since we worked closely together in the past, I'd be honored if you'd provide a professional reference. Your great reputation in the industry would help to verify my credentials. Will you help?

REFERENCE: I'd be delighted. Do you need a letter, or do you just want me to be on the ready for phone calls?

JOB SEEKER: I'm not sure yet. But I'll send you a copy of my resume today, along with a brief summary of the work we did together on the _____ project, just to refresh you. I'll also include a list of questions you might be asked. I'll get it all out to you in the next day or two.

RFERENCE: Great! When do you expect these calls to start coming in?

JOB SEEKER: I'm not sure. I haven't lined up any interviews yet, but I'll drop you a note when I do, with names of companies I'm considering.
REFERENCE: OK. I'll talk to you soon. And good luck.

The call to a personal reference, a neighbor, for instance, might go like this:

JOB SEEKER: Howard, this is Betty Brown.
REFERENCE: Hi, Betty. I've been meaning to call and ask you what you're using on your roses this year. They look great.
JOB SEEKER: Why thank you. I'll have to refer that question to the family gardener. Frank takes care of the yard.
REFERENCE: What can I do for you today?
JOB SEEKER: Well, I just passed the CPA exam, and I want to make a career move. Foster Plastics is a great company, and it was convenient to work in town while the kids were young, but now I'm ready for a larger organization. I thought I'd target the insurance industry.
REFERENCE: I wish I knew someone to recommend. I'm afraid I can't be much help.
JOB SEEKER: You can be a big help. I'd like to use your name as a personal reference. When we worked together on last year's school budget campaign, I was impressed by your energy, your effectiveness, and your ability to communicate. I hope your observations of me were equally good, and that you wouldn't mind saying so in a letter.
REFERENCE: I'm honored to be asked! I couldn't have accomplished what I did without your assistance in supplying the numbers to support our arguments. The Board of Ed is still talking about the accuracy of your projections.
JOB SEEKER: If you'd put those thoughts into a short letter for me, I'd be most appreciative. With your power of expression, I can't lose.[1]

Step 2: Provide Background Information

Each person should receive a reference packet that includes:

• Information about who might call, from what company, and about what position.
• A completed job application (if relevant).
• A copy of your resume (consult Chapter 5 for tips on preparing chronological and functional resumes).

---

[1] Jeffrey G. Allen, *The Perfect Job Reference* (New York: John Wiley & Sons, 1990), p. 54.

•   A summary of your professional accomplishments and personal attributes that are relevant to the target job (see Figures 7.3 and 7.4).

•   A list of questions they might be asked during a telephone reference check. Provide two versions: one blank and one with suggested answers to help them remember (see Figures 7.5 and 7.6).

Step 3: Follow up

Always recontact your references after they've acted on your behalf to express your gratitude and to get their impression of your prospective employer—and your prospects.

HOW TO GET A REFERENCE WHEN YOUR EMPLOYER KNOWS YOU'RE LEAVING

If you've embarked on a job search with your current employer's blessings, negotiate a favorable reference *before* you leave. Then type a letter on company stationery that emphasizes the positive aspects of your tenure and prepare it for the signature of the highest ranking, most genuinely interested person you can find. People dread writing reference letters but sign them willingly.

SITUATION ANALYSES

Situation No. 1

Marilyn G., a court reporter, applies for a job that requires traveling to different law offices every day. She is in a wheelchair but is able to drive and maneuver in the chair independently.

During the interview, the manager asks to call her present employer for a reference. She has an excellent reference letter from the employer, but she is concerned that in a phone call the employer will reveal that she has been getting progressively weaker from rheumatoid arthritis.

Does the ADA prevent the manager from contacting Marilyn's present employer? Does it at least prevent any discussion of her disability? Can she insist that the prospective employer accept her doctor's prognosis? Can she insist that the company's doctor examine her? If the manager consents, is the company required to hire her upon the recommendation of its doctor?

Analysis.   Nothing in the ADA prohibits contacting an employer for a reference, but it does prohibit discussing an applicant's medical condition before an offer is extended.

Marilyn has no right to insist that her doctor's prognosis be accepted without question. She probably has the right to a company-paid physical

Figure 7.3   The Professional Reference Summary

Name: John R. Smith   Tel No.: (917) 321-8732

Former Title: National Sales Manager

Accomplishments

- Supervised and motivated a field sales force that grew from 12 people to 20 during three-year tenure. Managed and led in-house sales support staff of six.

- Set and monitored sales objectives by territory and product, resulting in an average annual increase in sales of 30 percent, with an overall three-year cumulative increase of 120 percent (from $6 million in 1980 to $13.2 million in 1983).

- Purchased and installed computerized sales monitoring and reporting system.

- Used customer feedback to help create and market three new products—the Accu Soft, the Accu Sort, and the Accu Scan—which are consistently among the top sellers produced by the company.

- Established a sales incentive program that increased sales across the board and more than 50 percent in each of the two lowest performing territories.

   Traits: • Fast moving, effective, results oriented.
            • Highly skilled at motivating others to achieve their goals.
            • Reliable, loyal, enthusiastic.

Source: Reprinted with permission from Jeffrey G. Allen, *The Perfect Follow-up Method to Get the Job*. New York: John Wiley & Sons, 1992, p. 106.

Figure 7.4   The Personal Reference Summary

Name: Betty R. Brown   Telephone No. (616) 522-3359

Position Desired: Accountant, Insurance Company

Character Traits

- Determination
- Accuracy
- Thoroughness
- Commitment
- Follow through
- Energy
- Enthusiasm
- Competence
- Positive attitude

Job-Related Abilities and Skills

- Compiled financial data and developed complete, accurate forecasts.
- Presented concise, understandable financial reports for budget projections.
- Knowledge of accounting principles and procedures.

Source: Reprinted with permission from Jeffrey G. Allen, *The Perfect Follow-up Method to Get the Job.* New York: John Wiley & Sons, 1992, p.108.

Figure 7.5   The Professional Reference Questions List

How long have you known _____ ?

How do you know _____ ?

When was he/she hired? _____

When did he/she leave? _____

What was his/her salary when he/she left? _____

Why did he/she leave? _____

Did you work with him/her directly? _____

Was he usually on time? _____

Was he/she absent from work very often? _____

Did his/her personal life ever interfere with his/her work? _____

What were his/her titles? _____

What were his/her duties? _____

Did he/she cooperate with supervisors? _____

Did he/she cooperate with coworkers? _____

Did he/she take work home very often? _____

What are his/her primary attributes? _____

What are his/her primary liabilities? _____

Is he/she eligible for rehire? _____

Can you confirm the information he/she has given? _____

Source: Reprinted with permission from Jeffrey G. Allen, *The Perfect Follow-up Method to Get the Job*. New York: John Wiley & Sons, 1992, p. 107.

Figure 7.6   The Personal Reference Questions List

How long have you known _____ ?

How do you know _____ ?

_____

What is your opinion of _____ ?

_____

_____

_____

Does he/she get along well with others? _____

Is he/she usually on time? _____

Is he/she absent from work very often? _____

Does he/she bring work home very often? _____

Does he/she like his/her job? _____

What are his/her primary attributes? _____

_____

_____

_____

What are his/her primary liabilities? _____

_____

_____

Source: Reprinted with permission from Jeffrey G. Allen, *The Perfect Follow-up Method to Get the Job.* New York: John Wiley & Sons, 1992, p. 109.

by a company-appointed doctor. She can also reasonably request a review of her doctor's findings.

While the company is not bound by its doctor's report, Marilyn will have the basis for filing a charge of discrimination. Ultimately, a third opinion might be sought from an independent medical examiner.

Situation No. 2

Leslie R. is a finance company officer who walks with an artificial leg. The firm she works for was recently acquired by a major insurance company, and she must now attend monthly meetings out of town. She has asked the employer to let her attend the meetings by telephone, but her request was denied.

Leslie just learned she will be fired for "lack of production." This is a smoke screen, as she has consistently met her performance goals over a period of years. The company will not use the actual reason for termination because it recently lost a major discrimination case brought by a disabled employee.

Should Leslie disclose the real reason for her termination when she applies for employment? What if the employer gives another reason on a reference check?

Analysis. The ADA prohibits discrimination in employment based on a disability, and that's just what Leslie's employer is doing.

However, 13 states also recognize the theory of "compelled self-publication" in the job reference area. Where it applies, an employer who fabricates a reason for termination is liable if the former employee is forced to state that reason. Compelled self-publication is a form of defamation— *libel* if it's written, and *slander* if it's oral. The employer is subject to *unlimited liability* because defamation is *intentional tort* (civil wrong).

This employer would even be liable under the compelled self-publication theory if it used a neutral reference policy that confirmed only the former employee's name, last job title, and dates of employment. While employers think they're protecting themselves through this limited verification, it invites liability under the same compelled self-publication theory.

In this case, the employer's wrongdoing is both a discriminatory practice as it applies to Leslie and a civil wrong as it applies to former employees generally. Thus, Leslie may be able to file a charge with the Equal Employment Opportunity Commission (EEOC) based upon the discriminatory employment practice and also pursue civil litigation privately.

Situation No. 3

Michael P. is a senior computer troubleshooter. He was considered a key employee for over a decade, but then he developed emphysema. His illness makes it impossible for him to work in certain factories and urban locations where there is air pollution.

Michael often doesn't know where he will be dispatched. Because of the air quality at certain sites, he has been unable to complete some of his emergency service calls. Now he is on probation for failure to perform his assignments and excessive absenteeism.

Michael wants to find a job where he won't have these problems, but he is concerned that the reference from his last job will be poor. Does the ADA protect him? What can he do to stop walking around under a reference rain cloud?

Analysis. It seems unreasonable (and unlawful) for the employer to use this disability as a basis for firing Michael, since there appear to be some simple alternatives. For instance, someone could readily screen service calls in advance as to air quality, or Michael could review the list of customers in advance.

If the employer tries to interfere with his future employment, Michael could file a charge of discrimination seeking reinstatement to his former job, service call screening, back pay, and compensation for any other losses he sustained.

The EEOC is empowered to investigate anything "like or related to a charge of discrimination," so this employer is in big trouble. If he handles it properly, Michael will get good references. The sun is shining already.

CHAPTER EIGHT

The BIG Question: Should I Disclose?

Questions of whether or not to disclose your disability to a prospective employer and when to do so are pivotal. Unfortunately, there are no pat answers. It is a personal decision that has to be made for each job lead you pursue based on the nature of your disability and on what you know about the employer. The bottom-line consideration should be: *Does disclosure of my disability at this time support my objective of getting hired?* If it doesn't, don't do it. But if it does, think strategically about when and how to present your disability in a positive light.

Even though the law says you don't have to discuss your disability with a prospective employer except as it relates to your ability to perform essential job functions, in reality you probably won't get the job if you don't open up. Your willingness to discuss your disability candidly shows a strength of character that makes you equal to most any task. It's a question of packaging and presentation. You don't just say, "Oh, by the way, I'm disabled." You make an affirmative statement that presents your disability not as a problem, but as a selling point.

DISCLOSURE TIMING OPTIONS

There are several junctures in the job search process at which you can disclose a disability. These include:

- In a third-party reference letter or call
- On the resume

- In your cover letter
- When the employer calls to set up an interview
- On the employment application
- At the interview
- After you have been offered the job
- After you start work
- Never

Through Third-Party Reference

In my book *The Perfect Job Reference*, I explained the power of credible references. A strong reference letter from a former employer, colleague, trade association official, or vendor can help you get a foot in the door, especially if the person has impressive credentials in his or her field.

Unless you ask them not to, your references will probably mention your disability when talking to a prospective employer, so think about how you want them to handle the subject *before* they write or call in your behalf. It's not unreasonable for you to want some input on this issue. If nothing else, you need to make sure that they have accurate information about your disability and are using the proper medical terminology for it. If you are uncertain as to how your disability will be presented, it's better to have your references write instead of call. That way, you can offer to draft the letter yourself for their signature or ask to review it before it is sent.

On Resume

In some cases, a disability is woven into the fabric of a person's professional life. Rather than trying to conceal it, use that experience to reveal your disability in a positive light. For instance, if your work history includes five years' employment at an agency for the blind, any attempt to conceal that fact would create a noticeable time gap and could work against you.

You can also provide broad hints at a disability on your resume by noting your involvement in organizations or advocacy projects. Again, this places it in a positive context. Don't include a section titled "Health" on your resume—and never mention your disability under that section.

In Cover Letter

Sometimes it is to your advantage to discuss your disability openly in a cover letter. If you are applying for a position as a braille proofreader, a peer counselor for people with burn injuries, or a rehab counselor, it would be a good idea to mention your disability. On the other hand, some companies recruit people with disabilities because they have to meet affirmative action goals or because they have federal contracts. In this case, there is no guarantee that your disability gives you an advantage in applying. A boilerplate statement such as "XYZ Corporation is an affirmative action employer" doesn't gauge a company's true commitment to employing workers with disabilities.

If you disclose in a cover letter, compose a one-page letter in which you:

1. Disclose the fact that you are disabled.
2. Describe succinctly how you can perform the work in question; emphasize that you are adaptable and learn quickly.
3. Indicate that you are aware of attitudinal barriers in the workplace and explain how you plan to help your coworkers feel more comfortable with your disability.
4. Mention your desire to be treated as an equal and to be evaluated according to the same standards as others.
5. Emphasize that you never trade on your disability.
6. Mention that you have references (don't give names yet) who can vouch for your job performance and attendance.

Attach the letter to the *back* of your resume so that the employer can focus on your qualifications without any preconceptions.[1]

On Employment Application

Some organizations require all jobseekers, even those at management levels, to fill out a standard employment application. If the form asks, "Do you have any physical limitations that would hinder your performance in the position applied for?" you could use this as an opportunity to disclose. However, this is probably not the ideal forum because it does not allow you much leeway to elaborate. The important thing to remember when confronted with this question is *perspective*. What matters is whether *you* believe you can do the job, not whether the *employer* believes it. And remember, it doesn't matter that you have a disability as long as it will not prevent you from performing the job in question. If you're not sure how it would affect your job performance, you can write "will discuss."

Some companies are now using a standardized voluntary disclosure form like the one shown in Figure 8.1 for job applicants as well as current employees. The form can double as both a disclosure statement and a

[1]Rami Rabby and Diane Croft, *Take Charge: A Strategic Guide for Blind Job Seekers* (Boston: National Braille Press, 1989), Chap. 3.

**Figure 8.1   Voluntary Disclosure of Disability and Request
for Accommodations**

XYZ Company policy and the law prohibit the company from asking job applicants about disabilities or giving a health questionnaire or examination until after an initial job offer is made. Whether you are a job applicant or a current employee, you may want to *voluntarily* disclose physical or mental health conditions and ask for reasonable accommodations so that the company may consider possible changes that allow you to work at your full potential.

If you choose to do so, please complete and sign this form and return it to _____ . Information given on this form, or the failure to complete this form, will not be used to discriminate against you. The information will remain strictly confidential. Disclosure will be made only to those people who are needed to determine and implement reasonable accommodations.

The company is strongly committed to taking all reasonable steps to ensure that qualified applicants are hired and qualified employees are allowed to work to their full potential, despite physical or mental problems.

For the purposes of this form, a potential disability appropriate for disclosure is any physical or mental condition that creates, or might create, any difficulty in performing your job. This includes obvious disabilities such as paralysis or blindness; less obvious impairments such as epilepsy, diabetes, or heart problems; mental problems such as depression and eating disorders; learning problems such as dyslexia. Also included as impairments are acquired immunodeficiency syndrome (AIDS), human immunodeficiency virus (HIV), and other contagious diseases; persistent back problems; past drug addiction; past or current alcoholism; and other medical conditions.

$$*\quad*\quad*$$

Name _____

Position Applied for or Currently Held _____

Type of Disability (e.g., diabetes, amputation, cancer, high blood pressure)

_____

_____

Description of Physical or Mental Impairment (e.g., unable to walk, cannot do heavy lifting, sensitive to heat) _____

_____

_____

Suggested Accommodations (e.g., ramp over stairs, telephone amplifier, flexible work schedule) _____

_____

Figure 8.1   (*Continued*)

The company will consider your suggestions and attempt to make reasonable accommodations. However, the final decision regarding what accommodations are reasonable and desirable remain the sole discretion of the company. Please sign below.

Signed _____   Date _____

Source: From pp. 194–195 of the *Employer's Guide to the Americans with Disabilities Act* by James G. Frierson. Copyright © 1992, by The Bureau of National Affairs, Inc., Washington, DC 20037. Reprinted with permission.

request for a job accommodation. Note that it gives examples of specific disabilities but allows the individual to explain the nature of his or her disability.

When Employer Calls for an Interview

If you decide not to disclose in your resume or cover letter, you can still do so in advance of the interview. Many people find that the most natural time to disclose a disability is when the employer calls to arrange an interview. After scheduling a date and time, ask if the caller is the person who will interview you. If so, you might say something like: "I want to mention before we meet that I use a walker to get around. I'm generally able to navigate stairs and elevators, so getting to your office shouldn't be a problem. I'll be glad to answer any questions about how my mobility relates to the job during our interview." Because the employer has already committed to meeting with you, it would be openly discriminatory to cancel the interview in light of your disclosure.

On the other hand, if the person who calls to schedule the interview is a secretary or assistant, *don't say anything about your disability*. You want to discuss this matter in your own words with the interviewer or manager, not have it paraphrased and possibly distorted by someone else. In this case, you will have to find out who will interview you and place a separate phone call directly to that person.

Employers participating in an informal survey conducted by the authors of *Take Charge: A Strategic Guide for Blind Job Seekers* were unanimous in feeling that they want to know about an applicant's physical limitations—especially an obvious one such as blindness—before the interview. They maintain that the "shock factor" instills an attitude of mistrust and defensiveness. If the interviewer is not prepared in advance, time is wasted adjusting to the situation, and the disability becomes a major distraction.[2]

A lot of jobseekers agree. "I've always believed that a prospective employer should know up front that I have a visual disability," says Marilyn Rosenthal, former deputy assistant counsel to the governor of New Jersey, blind since childhood.[3]

At Interview

Although employers prefer to know about a disability in advance of the interview, jobseekers are divided on the subject.

Some prefer not to say anything until they arrive at the interview so that the employer can evaluate them on the strength of their qualifications, not on their disability. "Why should I mention my disability?" asks one man. "That just gives employers more time to rationalize their fears about hiring me."

Others are wary about the shock treatment. An interviewer might resent being caught off guard and react with embarrassment or even hostility. There's also a question of trust. One employer maintains that "I couldn't trust someone who would withhold information that might have an impact on the job."

If you can use the shock value to your advantage and then put the interviewer at ease, this delayed disclosure strategy can be very effective. You need good interpersonal skills and a sense of showmanship to pull it off.

After Job Offer

If your disclosure at this point changes the hiring decision, you may be entitled to take legal action (see Chapter 14). If you wait until the postoffer phase, you risk the employer's resenting the fact that you didn't mention it earlier.

After Starting Work

This strategy gives you an opportunity to prove yourself on the job. You can feel more confident about disclosing your disability once you have

---

[2]Ibid.

[3]Marie Attmore, comp. *Career Perspectives: Interviews with Blind and Visually Impaired Professionals* (New York: American Foundation for the Blind, 1990), 2.

earned the support and recognition of your supervisor and coworkers. The disadvantage of waiting until this time is that you may not be able to do the job well until the necessary accommodations have been made. Your disability may have already impacted your performance.

Choosing Not to Disclose

Sometimes it's best to say nothing. If you have a record of a disability but are no longer disabled, don't bring it up. If you have an invisible disability that will not affect any essential functions of your job and will not require an immediate accommodation, you need not—and probably should not— say anything. On the other hand, if you're going to need an accommodation, you have no choice but to reveal your disability. Employers can't meet your needs if they don't know what they are. If you don't disclose a disability, you could experience tension on the job from lack of support. It might even aggravate your condition.

WHAT EMPLOYERS CAN'T ASK

Although the ADA doesn't prevent employers from seeking the information they need to evaluate a job candidate, it does restrict the scope and purpose of their questioning. As noted in Chapter 2, medical examinations are not permitted at the preemployment phase in the hiring process. During this period, employers may not make *any* inquiries about disabilities, absenteeism, illness, or worker's compensation history.

The law categorically prohibits "fishing" for information about a candidate's physical or mental condition—either on an application form or during an interview, either formally across the desk or informally over lunch. *An employer may inquire only about a person's ability to perform specific job-related functions.*

Example _____

If you are interviewing for a maintenance position, the employer cannot ask, "How did you lose your arm?" He or she may, however, ask you to explain or demonstrate how you would use certain tools in that job.

The ADA prohibits employers from asking the following types of questions:

- Have you ever been treated for the following listed conditions or diseases?
- Has anyone in your family ever had any of the following listed illnesses?

- Have you ever been hospitalized? For what?
- List any conditions or illnesses for which you have been treated in the past three years.
- Have you ever been treated for a mental disorder?
- Are you taking any medication?
- Have you ever been treated for drug addiction or alcoholism?
- Do you have any major physical disabilities?
- If so, how did your disability come about? What is the prognosis for recovery?
- Have you ever filed for worker's compensation benefits?
- How many times were you absent from your previous job because of illness?
- Do you have any disabilities that would affect your performance in the position for which you are applying?

WHAT EMPLOYERS CAN ASK

In general, employers can still ask questions related to essential job functions and to your prior job responsibilities. If you request an accommodation, they can ask what you will need to perform the job. Following are examples of the types of specific questions that an employer is allowed to ask a job applicant with disabilities:

- Can you lift a 50-pound box?
- Can you stand (or sit) for an extended period of time?
- Can you be at work by 9:00 A.M. every day?
- Can you work five days a week?
- Can you reach the top of a six-foot-high filing cabinet?
- Do you have a driver's license?
- Can you perform the job for which you are applying with or without an accommodation?
- What were your duties on your previous job and what accommodations were made to facilitate your work?
- Show me how you would perform a particular job task.

Employers may also require preemployment drug tests and postoffer medical examinations as long as they are given across the board to all new hires (see Chapter 2).

FINDING THE COMFORT ZONE

One jobseeker summed it up this way:

> *You're not going to get the job if you make the interviewer uncomfortable. But my argument is that if they are uncomfortable when*

they see you, they're going to be uncomfortable, period. They may act better if they have time to prepare, but that doesn't mean they'll hire you. The person who ultimately hires you is the one who feels comfortable with you and asks questions about your disability. [4]

You want the interviewer to feel comfortable discussing your disability, but you also want to strike a balance with your own self-respect. Sometimes you have to decide whether you want the job badly enough to answer questions about how you dress in the morning or go to the bathroom.

SITUATION ANALYSES

Situation No. 1

Joan T. wants to apply for a manager's job in an upscale mall dress shop. She has an artificial leg but has used the mall ramps effectively.

When Joan applies for the job, the manager notices her limp and asks about it. Joan tells her she has an artificial leg. The manager informs her that the job involves a lot of standing and walking.

Joan fills out an application. She doesn't disclose her disability on the form because she knows she can do the job by using a bar stool behind the counter, and she thinks the manager didn't note her disability on the application.

Joan has been invited for an interview at the corporate personnel office. Must she notify the interviewer in advance about her disability? Must she mention it during the interview? Can the interviewer ask about her limp? Can she be denied the job because the company doesn't want a manager sitting behind the counter?

Analysis. Let's answer these questions in order:

1.   Joan is under no duty to inform the interviewer in advance about her disability. Why risk the chance of rejection?
2.   Joan is also under no duty to mention the disability during the interview. However, this seems to be an appropriate time to do so because she needs a minor alteration in the workplace—a bar stool.
3.   The interviewer can probably ask about the limp because it might impinge upon Joan's ability to do the job. If she were applying for a desk job, it probably would not be appropriate to ask.
4.   The interviewer can't deny Joan the job. The difference between stand-

---

[4]Rabby and Croft, *Take Charge*, 130.

ing and perching behind a counter is hardly a legitimate business concern. Nondisabled employees can still be required to stand.

Situation No. 2

Mark C. has been hired as an engineer and has been asked to take a routine company physical examination. He has a severe heart condition and is afraid he'll be fired if the physical discloses it.

Does he have to take the physical, or can he submit a report from his own doctor instead? Can he be fired if the heart condition is discovered? Must the company's group insurance carrier cover him for the preexisting condition?

Analysis. Again, let's take the questions one by one:

1. Mark is under no legal obligation to take the company physical because it's not a "business necessity."
2. If his doctor believes the report and records will demonstrate no reason for concern, Mark should consider this alternative. However, it's unclear whether he is waiving his ADA right to prevent a medical inquiry by this disclosure. I'd be inclined to advise against it.
3. Mark can't be fired if his heart condition is discovered. The employer assumed the risk by not asking about it at the preemployment phase. Even at that point, inquiries are restricted to job-related issues.
4. The group insurance carrier is probably bound to cover the preexisting condition, too. In the absence of some written misrepresentation by Mark to conceal his condition, he'll be covered.

Situation No. 3

Phillip E., a senior mechanical engineer, has a mysterious heart disorder that could result in sudden death. The cause is unknown, and it can't be treated with any known surgery, medicine, or therapy. A cardiologist commented that Phillip is "a walking time bomb."

Other than his heart condition, Phillip is in perfect health. He just passed a routine preemployment physical. He answered the medical history questionnaire honestly, but it didn't cover his condition.

Now that Phillip is ready to report for work, must he tell the employer about his problem? Does he have a duty to do so for his own physical safety? Can the employer give him short, low-priority projects even though he is technically qualified for major ones?

Analysis. Phillip is not legally obligated to report his heart condition. He did not falsify the medical history questionnaire or any other employment document. In fact, he doesn't even have a disability under the ADA because his condition is not "a physical or mental impairment that substantially limits one or more major life activities."

Phillip's physical safety is a personal matter. If he wants to tell trusted coworkers once he's on the job, fine. Otherwise, let's wish him a long, happy, productive life.

Note: This is an actual case. I sent Phillip a T-shirt from one of our temp service clients that reads "Life is a temporary assignment." He laughed.

CHAPTER NINE

Interviewing Guidelines

A job is not won by qualifications alone. The general impression you make during a single 30- to 60-minute performance determines the outcome of your job search. Everything you've done up until now—networking, writing a resume, getting references, researching employers—is a prelude to this performance.

Employers generally look for three qualities in a job candidate: enthusiasm, integrity, and intelligence. For the job candidate with a disability, there is a fourth, but unspoken, criterion: self-sufficiency. In addition to the usual anxieties surrounding the event, you must think about how the interviewer will react to your disability and how you can project an image of capability. You must convince the interviewer not only that are you the best person for the job but that your disability will not impinge upon your performance.

The interview is a stressful situation, but it is also a rehearsable, predictable, and controllable event. The guidelines presented in this chapter, drawn from my book *Jeff Allen's Best: Win the Job*, are relevant for *all* jobseekers who are preparing for a first interview with a company. The question of how to handle disclosure of a disability during an interview is discussed at length in Chapter 8 on disclosure strategies.

HOW THE PROCESS WORKS

There are basically two types of initial interviews:

- The *screening interview*, designed to weed out unqualified candidates right at the gate. These interviews are usually conducted by human re-sources staff within the company or an outside recruiter. Screeners don't make hiring decisions, they merely pass on qualified candidates to hiring managers. As a rule of thumb, it is best to hold your cards close to the chest in this situation. This is not the place to reveal your personality or your personal beliefs.

•   The *selection interview*, where hiring managers meet with prescreened applicants to assess their qualifications in more detail. You are likely to be questioned about your work style, background, and attitudes to determine if you are compatible with the manager and the general office environment. Personality counts in this situation.

In some small companies, the screener and the hiring manager are the same person. The manager's assistant or secretary might help with the initial screening.

PREPARING YOURSELF MENTALLY

Schedule for Success

Scheduling is one aspect of the interviewing process over which you *can* exert some control. When you set up interviews at random times, your energy level, attention span, and response time may vary widely. Consistent scheduling will give you the winner's edge. When your body chemistry is in the same balance each time, your delivery is more consistent, your nervous system is stabilized, and you feel more confident.

You also want to strike a balance between your best time and the interviewer's. The advice for timing the arrival of your resumes and cover letters—to avoid Monday mornings and Friday afternoons—applies here as well.

Limit Interviews to 45 Minutes

The 45-minute time limit is critical. If the interview drags beyond that, you risk losing focus and straying into unwelcome areas of discussion. Tell the interviewer you have another appointment. Even if you don't, you can use the time more productively to reflect on your performance and prepare your follow-up strategy. Here, again, you do have some control over timing.

Do Your Homework

If you develop a profile of each company you interview with, you can boost your confidence during the interview and impress an employer with your initiative. You can use the information you acquire through your research to mention the employer's successes at appropriate places in the interview.

Refer back to Chapter 6, Job Leads, for sources to use in gathering market intelligence and suggested questions to ask.

A company's vital statistics are fine for background, but an understanding of the "corporate culture" is even more important in an interview situation. If you portray yourself as an autocratic manager when the company encourages team decision making, you'll be a mismatch no matter what your qualifications are. You might get a better sense of an organization's personality if you do some of your research by phone.

Rehearse

There's no substitute for practice. Practice with your voice. Speak your lines out loud so you can hear your inflections, volume, diction, and tone. Breathe from your diaphragm and enunciate clearly. Listen for annoying speech habits. Also rehearse your answers. Anticipate tough questions and have your responses fixed in your mind. (Some common interviewing questions and sample responses are included in the next chapter.)

If you're really serious about perfecting your delivery, stage mock interviews with friends and relatives. Wear your dress uniform and videotape your performance. That way you can check your overall look as well as your body language: posture, nervous mannerisms, eye contact, facial expression, hand gestures, etc.

Get Your Support System in Place

If you need a driver or someone to help you dress for the interview, make sure the person knows the schedule for the day. You will have enough to think about without having to deal with "support system anxiety."

Russ Conte, an employment specialist and recruiter for Chicagoland Project with Industry, advises those who are going to use an interpreter in an interview to make sure the person is familiar with the words and concepts in your industry. You might have to do some serious coaching and rehearsal if you want your interpreter to do justice to your knowledge. Although Conte often assists hearing-impaired clients in interviews, he acknowledges that he does not have the vocabulary to converse in certain highly specialized technical fields.

PREPARING YOURSELF PHYSICALLY

Dress the Part

Like it or not, appearance is important in our culture. A well-groomed, well-dressed person automatically commands respect. Well dressed in the context of a job interview means *understated*. The interview is no time to make a fashion statement. You want to be remembered for your skills and character—not your costume. You can minimize the visual impact of your disability if you know the business uniform and wear it proudly. Select clothing that works with your disability: comfortable, durable, with simple lines neatly tailored to your body contours.

Even though Russ Conte places high-end professionals, he notes that many people with disabilities don't have a lot of money to spend on clothes. "Resale shops and Goodwill stores are great places to find good dress shirts, ties, and suits that can look like new with a cleaning, pressing, and starching," he says. "Clothes can be altered to your disability; they don't have to be custom-made."

Of course, there are clothing manufacturers that do specialize in fashions for people with disabilities. One is Avenues (1199 Avenida Acaso, Suite K, Camarillo, CA 93012), which markets a line of clothing for people who use wheelchairs. Call 800/848-2837 to order a free catalog.

The bottom line is not fashion, but grooming. You must look clean and in control of your body.

• Your hair should be clean, combed, and conservatively cut. Short styles are best for men and women. Keep sprays and hair dressings to a minimum.
• Nails should be trimmed. A light or clear polish is acceptable for women, but long, blood-red or shocking pink nails make you look frivolous or predatory.
• Beards are generally not a plus in the business world, but if you wear one, keep it trimmed short.
• Jewelry should be limited to a watch, wedding band, or school ring. Leave service pins and religious or fraternal jewelry at home. Small earrings or a pin are acceptable for women.
• Avoid too much of anything: too much makeup, too much perfume, too much hair.

Interviewing Uniform for Men

When going on an interview, men should wear:

• Dark (preferably navy blue) conservative two-piece business suit. Gray may be worn, but save it for the second interview.
• White long-sleeved dress shirt. Wear a fresh one for each interview.
• Dark striped tie. Here, too, dark blue is best. A contrasting color (like red) is acceptable, but the predominant color should be the same as your suit.
• Black dress shoes and dark socks. Almost any shoe style is acceptable as long as the shoes are polished and well heeled.

Interviewing Uniform for Women

Although there is more fashion flexibility for women, important guidelines still hold true for interviews:

• A conservative suit or dress in a dark-colored quality fabric. Hems should be no higher than knee length, and necklines should be discreet. A suit should be paired with a business blouse or tailored shirt.
• A simple, low-heeled shoe in a color that matches your clothes; neutral-colored hosiery.
• A small, inconspicuous handbag in a color that matches your shoes. Don't overstuff it.

It is possible to look both feminine and professional, but it takes practice to walk that fine line. Avoid outfits that are too flowery, too tight, too short, too low-cut, too cute, or too flashy. Keep long hair pinned up or back. Curls cascading below your collar give the wrong impression.

Carry Briefcase

For men and women alike, regardless of the position, a briefcase is a necessity. It should be neatly stocked with a pen, notepad, extra copies of your resume, a completed employment application, and samples of your written or published work, if applicable.

Arrive Alone

Leave family and friends at home—or at least outside the door. You want to show that you are independent and mobile. Guide dogs, of course, are appropriate.

Once you arrive, someone—perhaps the receptionist—will take you from the waiting area into the office. If you need assistance, let the escort know what you want—"May I take your arm?" or "Will you hold the door for me?"

Arrive on Time

Lateness suggests that you don't know how to manage your time. When you arrive late, you're forced to begin the interview with an apology, which places you in a subordinate role. If an emergency detains you, phone ahead to reschedule, but don't wait until the last minute to call.

Respect works two ways. You shouldn't have to wait more than a half hour for the interviewer. Even if it's an unavoidable, unintentional delay, you're better off not waiting. You'll be angry, irritable, and dropping from the psychomotor peak (the helpful stage fright) reached at the scheduled time.

Allow Time to Acclimate

If you have 20 or 30 minutes before your appointment, use the time to get your bearings. Survey the premises and read bulletin boards or building directories for information. Find disabled access routes, restrooms, and building amenities. With about 10 or 15 minutes to go, find a restroom where you can check yourself in the mirror and freshen up. Take a deep breath, relax, and practice your best smile.

Fuel Your Body

If possible, eat a light snack a few minutes before the interview. I find that peanut butter or cheese sandwich crackers are convenient to carry and contain just the right amount of carbohydrates, protein, and fiber to get you through the hour.

THINKING STRATEGICALLY DURING THE INTERVIEW

Use the "Magic Four" Hello

1. A genuine smile.
2. Direct eye contact.
3. A firm handshake.
4. The words, "Hi, I'm (first and last name). It's a pleasure meeting you."

Practice Your Handshake

The handshake is an important element in body language. If you have full use of your hands, develop a firm, warm shake—neither a shark nor a flounder. If you have a prosthesis or limited use of your hands, the interviewer may not know what to do, so you'll have to take the lead. Don't apologize; just do what's natural. If you can't shake hands, smile warmly and make direct eye contact as you introduce yourself.

Don't Address Interviewer by First Name

In your correspondence, telephone calls, and during the interview itself it should always be "Mr." or "Ms." If the interviewer addresses you by your first name, ask if you may reciprocate: "Mr. Carlson—may I call you John?"

Don't Assume Subordinate Role

It feels like the interviewer holds all the cards: You need a job, the employer has the power to give it to you. In reality, the employer needs a good worker as much as you need a good job, so treat the interview as a mutually beneficial exchange. Don't allow nervousness or embarrassment about your disability to push you into a submissive posture. Don't apologize if a chair has to be moved to make room for you or if you need minor assistance.

Assess Interviewer's Style

In those first few moments, while greetings are exchanged and places are taken, you must be alert for clues to the interviewer's personality. These clues will help you determine how to approach the subject of your disability—if at all. If the interviewer is the type of person who bases decisions on hard evidence, you'll have to use facts and figures to strengthen your case. A person who operates on instinct and feelings of rapport will probably want to discuss your disability candidly from a more personal perspective.

Most psychologists divide people into four basic personality types:

• *Outgoing and direct.* Very sociable, energetic, friendly, and self-assured. These people are usually busy juggling several things at once. They have to like you before they'll listen to you. That means you'll have to smile more, talk faster, and get right to the point.

• *Self-contained and direct.* Often called "directors," they are reserved, conservative, well-organized, goal- and bottom-line-oriented. To get along with this type, you must be all business and give the interviewer a lot of air space.

• *Self-contained and indirect.* These are thinkers and are likely to be found in analytical professions. They don't speak up, socialize, or editorialize. They go about their work quietly and they get it done properly. These people thrive on data but need time to analyze it. If you're pushy, they'll withdraw. To succeed with this type, give them air space during the interview. Answer questions directly and succinctly and volunteer as much information as they need to make a decision.

• *Outgoing and indirect.* Also known as "helpers," this type is warm and friendly but has trouble making decisions. It is important to establish rapport with people of this nature and to accentuate the *person* in personnel. The helper type won't question you openly about your abilities, so you'll have to take the lead in discussing your qualifications. If you don't, you may leave the interview with a friend but not a job.

Try typecasting a few of your friends and coworkers into these four profiles. Learn to pick up on subtle clues in their language and demeanor.

Pay Attention to Body Language

Just as subtle clues can help you peg an interviewer's basic personality type, your own mannerisms can tell as much about you as your resume.

Head scratching, knuckle cracking, clothes pulling, nail biting, hair touching, paper shuffling, rocking, slouching, slumping, leg or arm crossing, downcast eyes—all are clues to the inner you. Try to control your body during the interview.

A new book titled *Subtext: Making Body Language Work in the Workplace* (Viking/Penguin, $19.95) is a virtual road map to nonverbal cues. According to author Julius Fast, an interviewer who sits back with hands steepled at chest height or with fingers laced behind the head has confidence in you. If the interviewer clenches his or her hands, taps the side of the nose, then puts an index finger to the ear, you're being rejected.[1]

Align Yourself with Interviewer

People like people who are like themselves: We exhibit this powerful law of human motivation in our voting, selection of spouses and friends, and product purchases. A subtle way to establish physical rapport with the interviewer is to mirror his or her body language, facial expressions, eye movement, rate of speech, tone of voice, and breathing patterns. This takes practice, because there is a big difference between "mirroring" and "mimicking," between aligning and offending. You can also align by using linguistic passwords—the insider language of the industry.

Develop List of Success Phrases

Here are some of my favorites:
"Work is not only the way to make a living, it's the way to make a life."
"We must be self-made, or never made."
"People who succeed don't wait for opportunities, they create them."
"As long as you stand in your own way, everything seems to be in your way."
"I'm prepared to be rejected but determined to keep on trying."
Use these or others you like. Practice them until they sound natural, and you'll find your self-confidence increasing.

Use "Tie-Down" Technique

The tie-down is a questioning technique that's designed to elicit a series of affirmative responses that lead to the major yes regarding your hiring. The final decision is the sum total of all the yeses throughout the interview.
The most common tie-down questions are:

---

[1] Julius Fast, *Subtext: Making Body Language Work in the Workplace* (New York: Viking/Penguin, 1993).

Am I not?
Aren't you/we/they?
Doesn't he/she/it?
Don't I/you/we/they?
Hasn't he/she/it?
Haven't I/you/we/they?
Isn't he/she/it?
Isn't that right?
Shouldn't I/he/she/you/we/they/it?
Wasn't I/he/she/it?
Weren't you/we/they?
Won't I/he/she/you/we/they/it?
Wouldn't I/he/she/you/we/they/it?

Tie-downs can be used at the end of a statement:

- "My qualifications appear to fit the position you have open, *don't they?*"
- "My use of a wheelchair shouldn't present any problems on the job, *don't you agree?*

At the beginning of a statement:

- *"Don't you think* we'll work well together?"
- *"Wouldn't you* like to see how I can be of assistance?"

Within a statement:

- Now that we've had the opportunity to meet, *don't you think* I would fit well in the organization?
- When you budget is approved, *won't it* expedite production to have someone who understands the project the way I do?"

As with the other strategies discussed in this chapter, the tie-down questioning technique requires practice. Use it sparingly for best results.

Know What Questions to Ask

Employers expect a serious job candidate to have questions, not about lunch hours and vacations—those are for a subsequent meeting—but about the position and its responsibilities. You want to appear that you, too, are assessing the fit between the employer and yourself, and the best way to do that is to ask pointed questions of your own. Proper questioning helps you draw out the interviewer and align your answers to the areas he or she considers significant.

The average applicant talks about 85 percent of the time during an interview. That's why average applicants don't get hired. Try the following questions to get the interviewer talking:

How do you see the scope of this job?

What specific outcomes are expected of the position?

What are the most critical skills for this position?

Can you describe a typical day on this job?

Will I receive any training for the position?

To whom would I report?

Would I have any supervisory responsibilities?

What is the career path from this position?

What areas of the company does this department work most closely with?

When do you expect to make a hiring decision?

How long has the position been open?

How many people have held the position in the last five years?

Be Honest

You can't build a solid career on a foundation of lies. Even if your deception is never found out, you won't feel right about it. The other side of the honesty coin is knowing how to take credit for what you have done. When an interviewer says, "These are really impressive credentials," smile and say, "Thank you. Developing my career has been a rewarding challenge. I'd like to pursue the challenge at (name of company)."

Take Control of Disability Issue

When confronted with an obvious disability such as blindness, a lot of interviewers are hesitant to ask direct questions. They are usually thinking, "Do I say *disabled* or *handicapped*? Is it legal to ask how she'll get to work?"

In this case, you can get the upper hand by raising the issues yourself early on in the interview: "If you want to know how I'm going to do the job, just ask, and I'll gladly demonstrate what I can and can't do. Here's how I got to the office today.... Here's how I access print information.... Here are some of the adaptive devices I use in my work."

See Figure 9.1 for suggestions on how to discuss your disability with a prospective employer.

Keep Interview Focused on Your Qualifications

If you decide to bring up your disability during the interview, you must manage the discussion carefully. Keep it focused on work-related issues.

Figure 9.1   How to Discuss a Disability with Employers

- Plan what you will say before your interview with the manager.
- Be positive. Explain what you *can* do. Talk about your experience, education, and enthusiasm before you talk about special equipment or job modifications you will need.
- Try to make the interviewer comfortable with your disability.
- Be prepared to discuss the type and cost of any special equipment you will need. The Job Accommodation Network can provide you with this type of information.
- Don't be defensive about your disability.
- Be honest. Don't promise things you know you cannot accomplish.
- Keep the discussion focused on the job.

Source: *Arthritis and Employment*. Atlanta: Arthritis Foundation, October 1993.

You want to be open about the subject, but you don't want to spend the whole time talking about your disability. Chapter 8 on disclosure lists questions that employers can and cannot ask job candidates under the ADA. If an interviewer relentlessly pursues inappropriate topics, such as how you shop for groceries or prepare your meals, redirect the conversation to the potential contributions you could make to the organization. Although the temptation to do so is great, it is not a good idea to point out that such personal questions are illegal. You may be right, but you probably won't be hired.

Have Your References Ready

As the interview draws to a close, the employer will probably ask if you have any references who can speak to your qualifications. Be prepared with a neatly typed list of names, company affiliations, titles, addresses, and daytime phone numbers. If you have both personal and business references, list them separately.

Know Type of Job Accommodation You Will Need

Under the ADA, employers are obligated to provide "reasonable accommodations" to otherwise qualified job candidates with disabilities. They are not obligated to figure out *how* to accommodate a disability. If you are planning to discuss a job accommodation during your initial interview, try to have a clear idea of what you will need, where it can be obtained, and its approximate cost. Employers worry that accommodations are expensive, so anything you can do to allay that fear—including agreeing to share the cost of an accommodation—will go a long way to getting you hired.

We will discuss this key area of the ADA in detail in later chapters.

Close Interview on Area of Agreement

When you sense that the interview is winding down, move in for the close. Summarize your qualifications again and ask a direct question: "Do you see any gaps between my qualifications and the requirements for the position?" Answer the objections before you leave (and also make note of them for your follow-up letter) and close with a positive comment such as, "This is the kind of experience we need." Or try one of these responses as a way of closing out the interview:

"I'm excited about what I could do in this position."

"It sounds like the position was created for me."

"We seem to be a good match."

Use "Magic Four" Good-bye

1. A smile.
2. Direct eye contact.
3. A firm handshake.
4. The words, "I enjoyed talking to you. The position you have open sounds like a great opportunity. I look forward to hearing from you."

Interview Don'ts

- Don't smoke or chew gum.
- Don't wear dark glasses unless medically necessary.
- Don't interrupt.
- Don't look at your watch or gaze around the room. Give the interviewer your undivided attention.
- Don't take notes during the interview.
- Don't pick up any objects in the interviewer's office.
- Don't lie about your qualifications or your background.
- Don't tell the interviewer how many resumes you've sent out or how many interviews you've been on.
- Don't ask for the job.
- Don't be argumentative. Handle discriminatory questions politely and diplomatically.
- Don't play on the interviewer's sympathies. Compete on the strength of your skills.
- Don't discuss salary, benefits, or terms of employment. These matters are best left for a subsequent interview.
- Don't apologize—for anything!

FOLLOW-UP STRATEGIES

Giving your all in the interview is not enough. Follow-up correspondence, telephone calls, and networking are necessary to keep your candidacy alive.

Image the Interview

After the interview, get to a quiet place—even if it's only your car—and replay the scene in your head. Try to see yourself and the interviewer interacting, and rate your performance. Did you assess the person's style accurately? Did you align effectively? Did you ask intelligent questions? Did you receive positive feedback?

Also take time to write down any pertinent facts about the organization: names and titles of key individuals, details about products or services, future plans, and the like. You might be able to use this information in your follow-up letters, subsequent interviews, and salary negotiations. A sample interview recap form is shown in Figure 9.2.

Write Follow-up Letter

The things you say in an interview and the overall impression you make fade quickly from an employer's mind. The follow-up letter is the most effective postinterview technique you can use to keep yourself positioned out front. I'm not talking about a glorified thank-you note. A properly crafted letter takes what you learned in the interview and uses it to write sales copy that highlights your qualifications. Get it in the mail no more than three days after the interview.

Your interview follow-up letter should be as professional and polished looking as your initial cover letter: one page long, neatly typed in block format. You have only a small amount of space, so use it to your best advantage. Be brief, enthusiastic, and to the point. Accentuate your assets and accomplishments, and describe how you can benefit the employer. Include the properly spelled names of people you met and appropriate industry buzzwords. End with words similar to the magic four good-bye, requesting a reply as soon as possible.

Here is a sample format from my book, *How to Turn an Interview into a Job.* You can adapt the letter to the target job and personality of the interviewer.

1. **Address line**
    The full company name and address
    The interviewer's full name and title
2. **Subject line**
    Re: Interview for the Position of __(job title)__ on __(date)__

Figure 9.2   Interview Evaluation

Date and time of interview: _____

Name of company: _____

Address: _____

Phone: _____

Title of position available:_____

Duties: _____

Report to: (Name) _____ (Title) _____

Salary range: $_____

Bonus or other benefits: _____

Next career step: _____

Name of interviewer: _____

Title: _____

Personal characteristics of interviewer: _____

Interviewer's reaction to my disability: _____

Background information on company: _____

My qualifications for this position: _____

My weaknesses relative to the position: _____

Review of my interview performance: _____

Interviewer seemed most impressed by my: _____

My weakest areas during the interview were: _____

Follow-up letter sent to: _____ Date: _____

Follow-up calls made to: _____ Date: _____

Questions to ask in next interview: _____

3. **Greeting**
   Dear Mr./Ms.:
   First names are out of the question even if they were used during the interview.

4. **Opening**
   "It was a pleasure meeting with you last __(day)__ to discuss the opening in __(department)__ with Company X."

   or

   "Thanks again for taking the time to see me regarding the opening in __(department)__ ."

5. **Body**
   "From our discussion it appears that the position of __(job title)__ would allow me to make full use of my background in _____. I was particularly impressed with the professionalism of your organization. Company X has the kind of environment I have been looking for. The company seems to favor individual involvement, and I know I could contribute significantly to its goals."

6. **Closing**
   "It's an exciting opportunity, and I look forward to hearing your decision soon."

   or

   "Although I have been considering other situations, I have deferred a decision until I hear from you. Your prompt reply will help me make this important career step."

   or

   "The __(title of position)__ and Company X are exactly what I have been looking for in my career, and I hope to hear from you within the next week."

7. **Complimentary close**
   Sincerely,
   Very truly yours,
   Best regards,

Call Interviewer

If you haven't received a response to your follow-up letter within a week or so, pick up the phone, take a deep breath, smile, and call the interviewer. If you were interviewed by a manager rather than someone in personnel, enlist the support of the manager's secretary or assistant. Don't play guessing games to get around the front desk: An executive calling an executive always states his or her name. Say something like:

"Good morning, my name is (first and last name). Mr./Ms. (last name) and I met last week regarding the _____ position, and I want to follow up on our discussion."

Call References

After the interview, the employer will probably call your references to verify your credentials and learn more about you. Get there first. Call the people whose names you submitted and tell them about the job, how your qualifications fit it, and how the interview went.

Learn to Handle Rejection

Because the chances of landing the first job you apply for are slim, you have to learn to deal with rejection to keep going. Keep it in perspective, and don't take it personally. A rejection may mean that the interviewer had a bad day, that someone internally was shifted into the position you wanted, that the boss's brother-in-law needed a job, or that another candidate was more qualified. It should not affect your sense of self-worth.

SITUATION ANALYSES

Situation No. 1

Colleen E. is a very nervous lawyer waiting for her bar examination results. Her hearing is impaired intermittently, and hearing aids provide almost no assistance. Stress tends to make her condition worse, yet she wants to be a criminal defense attorney—one of the most stressful occupations known to man—or woman.

Colleen is scheduled to interview tomorrow with a major law firm, and she wants to be completely candid about her problem. She researched the ADA thoroughly and wants to cite specific provisions to make her case. How far should she go in her candor. Is it her responsibility to suggest "reasonable accommodations"? Must she accept limited activities as an entry level attorney?

Analysis. Colleen is too eager to disclose. She should at least wait until a second interview to discuss her problem. The probability of being rejected is much lower. The more interviews, the more likely an offer will be extended.

She is also overreacting to her disability. We're all disabled in some way. It's just that the law arbitrarily recognizes some disabilities and not others.

It's not Colleen's responsibility to suggest reasonable accommodations. More importantly, she hasn't been asked to do so.

Once she's on the job, the ADA will continue to protect her against discrimination. That should give the law firm an incentive to develop a mutually acceptable working arrangement.

Situation No. 2

Gail H. has been interviewing for over six months. She has an obivous speech impediment and has obtained no offers. She is qualified as an advertising layout specialist, and her speech doesn't interfere with her work.

But she can't get past the interview because success depends on verbal communication skills.

What can Gail do to get hired? Should she request a written interview? How about one that focuses on "doing" rather than "speaking"? What is the obligation of an employer to "reasonably accommodate" her requests?

Analysis. First, Gail should try using my book *The Complete Q&A Job Interview Book*. In it I give personalized interview scripts to prepare applicants for anything that might be asked.

If she can't adapt to this programmed technique, she can ask for a written interview, but that might be an awkward format for an interpersonal exchange. A skills test (laying out ad copy, for instance) would be a far more acceptable request.

Perfect speech doesn't seem to be an "essential function" of a layout job. Therefore, the ADA would require the employer to provide any reasonable accommodation to Gail for the interview—and the job.

Situation No. 3

Steve W. was formerly addicted to drugs but has successfully completed a rehabilitation program. He discussed this with the employer during his initial interview for a direct sales position.

The interviewer told Steve he probably wouldn't be selected because the stress of direct sales and the lack of supervision in the field might lead him to become addicted again.

Steve is upset. What should he do?

Analysis. Steve should relax. He has an equal right to the job.

However, in the future Steve should realize that there's no need to discuss his history with drugs. Like many who have conquered addiction, he is justifiably proud, but to an employer the mere mention of drugs is a threat.

There's a provision in the ADA that allows an employer to reject an applicant (or terminate an employee) if the job poses a "direct threat" to his or her health or safety. Although Steve might present a somewhat greater risk than another applicant without his history, he does not appear to present any imminent and direct danger to anyone, including himself. There are many civilized ways to monitor his performance.

CHAPTER TEN

The Second Interview: Negotiating Strategies

Employers today spend a lot of time and money checking and double-checking job applicants because they don't want to make costly hiring mistakes. They do it with everybody, not just people with disabilities. Applicants today are asked to take physical exams, drug tests, honesty tests, psychological tests—you name it—so don't be surprised if you are called back for several interviews. Even though the second interview is almost equated with getting the job, in this situation "almost" doesn't count.

You have a couple of inherent advantages in a second interview:

• You can go into it with more confidence, knowing that you've been doing something right up until now.
• You can prepare even more fully for your encore performance. Now you have not only your research notes to draw on but all the information you gained from your previous interview and follow-up contacts.

Don't assume that the second interview will be a replay of the first. In fact, it's sure to be different, although your basic approach will stay the same—alignment, tie-down questioning, finding areas of agreement, etc. In this case, though, you're likely to be talking to either a totally new team of interviewers or additional players on the original team. You can expect to be dealing with some first-string people this time out, as each interview is a screening process.

If your first interview was in the personnel department, you will often be asked to return for another meeting—this time with a department manager. If you already interviewed with a manager, you might be asked back to meet others in the department.

INTERVIEW FORMATS

Generally, the second interview is more directed. It takes one of two paths:

• *The "who are you?" interview.* This is similar to the first interview, with the interviewer asking probing questions about your background, character traits, work habits, skills, and outside interests. The difference is that now you have a clearer picture of your interviewer, the company, and the target job, so you can tailor your answers to fit the situation. Even though you're thinking strategically about your responses, the bottom line once again is honesty. You may have learned in your first interview that the manager is an opera buff, but if the opera bores you, why feign an interest?

• *The "what can you do for us?" interview.* This format tends to be informational rather than personal. Be prepared to demonstrate how your experience and skills will enable you to do the target job. Arm yourself with company information and technical data.

• *The mealtime interview.* If an employer invites you to breakfast, lunch, or dinner, beware: You are the main course on this menu. Your eating and drinking habits tell a lot about you, so mind your manners. If you don't know which forks or spoons to use, take a cue from your host.

Eat sensibly. Don't select either the most expensive item on the menu or the cheapest. Choose healthy foods, but don't be too prim. Select items that are easy to handle and chew. You have enough to think about without having to debone a Cornish hen.

Hide your habits. If you're a smoker, don't smoke unless your host does, and even then smoke sparingly if at all. If you're a drinker, don't drink. Order a nonalcoholic or very light drink before the meal; if wine is served with the meal, don't finish your glass. Even if your hosts are drinking heartily, don't join in.

WHAT FOLLOWS YES? POSTOFFER ISSUES AND STRATEGIES

Salary Negotiations

Whole books have been written on salary negotiation, so we won't try to cover the subject in a few pages here. Let's just pinpoint a few general guidelines.

As a rule of thumb, try to postpone any discussion of salary until you receive a firm job offer. By then you know the employer wants you, so you can bargain from a position of strength.

Employers have a clear advantage in salary negotiations because they know exactly what the job is worth to them, what their competitors are paying, and whether applicants for it are plentiful or scarce. Because the employer holds the cards in this situation, try to get him or her to name a figure first.

Negotiating a salary is similar to negotiating a loan: The more you appear to need it, the less likely you are to get it. Simply stated, the less you sweat, the more you get.

If you have to give a figure, use a range and aim near the top to give yourself leeway in negotiating. If you don't know what the range is, check the U.S. Department of Labor's wage and salary surveys at the public library, or Gale Research Company's *American Salaries and Wages.* To determine current salary ranges, add about 5 percent a year to salary figures, beginning with the year in which the data were gathered.

Don't oversell or undersell—that shows that you are either unreasonable or out of touch with the market. Salary is dependent not only on your individual qualifications but on overall supply and demand. If you're not a hot property, you probably won't be in a position to make nonnegotiable demands. Most employers start new hires near the bottom of the salary range for a position. In a nonunion setting, you have some room to negotiate; but in unionized companies or governmental agencies, the pay scale is determined collectively and hence is nonnegotiable.

If you do press for a higher starting salary, argue your case based on your qualifications, not on your personal financial needs. Don't set an adversarial tone: "I won't take the job for less than $25,000." Instead, be more tactful: "Your offer would be even more attractive if the salary were about . . . more." If the employer is firm on salary, press for an early review in six months, or ask for a small perk like a job-related seminar or a subscription to a professional publication.

The question of whether you should disclose your present salary is something you will have to decide for yourself. If you do, be sure to look beyond your paycheck stub. Don't state your present salary, per se. Instead, state the amount you will receive after your next review and the percentage increase you expect to receive. Don't forget to factor in overtime possibilities, bonuses, and accrued vacation time. Include the approximate monetary value of unusual perks—personal expense accounts, for instance—that the new employer is not offering. Don't falsify any information, but do be aware of the hidden amounts that can really add up.

If you don't want to answer a question about your present salary, try an evasive tactic like: "My previous salary was based on different job responsibilities." Or "I know we will reach an agreement on salary once we establish the scope of this position."

Salary isn't your only financial compensation. Keep in mind the company's total benefits package, which can amount to as much as one-third of a worker's annual salary. Fringe benefits are no longer fringes but a very substantial part of the pay package, especially with the skyrocketing costs of health care. One company might offer two weeks' vacation at the end of a year instead of only one. One might pay for your full health care coverage, whereas another might ask you to kick in each month. Some have profit-sharing and savings plans, others don't. It all adds up. Ask for a copy of the company's employee benefits handbook to give you the full picture.

Look Before You Leap

Just because you have a disability doesn't mean you have to grab at any job offer that comes along. In fact, if you do get an offer, play it cool and ask for a day or two to think about it. A lot can happen in that time: You might decide that the job isn't right for you; you might be called in for an interview at another company; you might even get another offer.

A job means more than a paycheck. It means working day in and day out with people whose personalities may or may not mesh with yours. It means working in a setting that may or may not be compatible with your personal style.

Ask yourself: Am I really interested in the duties I will be handling? Will this job make the best use of my skills? Is there an opportunity for advancement? Is this the kind of company I want to settle down with? Make sure you're clear about your job title, reporting authority, the scope of your duties, and travel or overtime demands. You may realize you forgot to nail down a particular fringe benefit, job accommodation, or other understanding. You must clarify these things *before* accepting the offer. All of the topics that were taboo in previous interviews are on the table now—vacation time, bonuses, health care coverage.

Never start a new job at a disadvantage. They'll never like you as much as they do at this minute, so use this opportunity to get what you need out of the job.

DO YOU NEED A CONTRACT?

Once the employer makes an offer, get it in writing to prevent costly misunderstandings down the line. The employer's company policy may prohibit negotiating formal employment contracts. Even so, you have other ways to delineate your job and protect yourself.

Letters of Agreement

Most companies send agreement letters as a matter of course; but if it isn't mentioned, say something like: "Your offer sounds great. When can you put it on paper and in the mail so that I can think it over?" The letter of offer should stipulate:

- Title
- Salary
- Benefits
- Job duties
- Starting date

This letter is the equivalent of an employment agreement. All you have to do to validate it is to respond in writing.

Send your response to the person who signed the offer letter, repeating the offer as stated and spelling out your understanding regarding key terms of employment. Your letter may contain any verbal changes made to the initial offer. A sample acceptance letter is shown in Figure 10.1.

Even if you're declining a job, do so in writing. Always be gracious and thankful for the opportunity. The world of work is surprisingly small and closely knit. You may meet these people again, and you want to think of them as allies.

Employee Handbook

Most employers have employee handbooks and/or written personnel policies. If you can't negotiate a written agreement, these documents serve as binding contracts between you and your employer. Ask to see this material before accepting a new position. It provides details about the job that an interviewer may gloss over. Personnel policy manuals are usually very specific about procedures for everything from phone usage to insurance.

Employment Contracts

It used to be that only top executives received formal employment contracts. Although such contracts are still reserved primarily for management positions, more and more employers are offering written contracts to new hires—not out of concern for the employee but as a way to protect themselves from litigation.

In *Perks and Parachutes*, author John Tarrant notes:

> *Written contracts are being offered in ever-increasing numbers to American white-collar employees. And while the most highly publicized contracts are given to board chairmen and chief executives, countless thousands of people in the middle management area are under contract today, or will be negotiating contracts soon. If you*

Figure 10.1   Sample Acceptance Letter

Date

Ms. Margaret O. Blaine
Product Manager
Convenience Foods Division
American Foods Company
1667 Commonwealth Avenue
Boston, Massachusetts 02210

Dear Ms. Blaine:

I am happy to accept your offer of employment in the position of assistant product manager at American Foods Company.

I understand that I will be responsible for the development, sales, and marketing of American's line of children's snack foods, supervising a staff of two and reporting to you.

The initial salary of $45,000 is agreeable to me, especially with your assurance of a bonus and a salary review within six months. The seasonal overtime you mentioned is manageable because it is predictable in June and July.

As I explained in our interview, my vision is limited due to cataracts, so I will require a large print video monitor for my workstation computer. The approximate cost of this equipment is $_____, which the company has agreed to pay as a reasonable job accommodation under the Americans with Disabilities Act.

As you suggested, I have read the American Foods employee handbook, and I am impressed by the company's policies regarding health insurance, vacation time, sick days, termination notice, and severance pay.

Since I have given notice at my current job, I will be able to start at American immediately after Thanksgiving. I look forward to seeing you then, and I am enthusiastically anticipating becoming a part of American Foods.

Sincerely,

Angela Edwards

Source: Adapted from Jeffrey G. Allen, *The Perfect Follow-up Method to Get the Job.* New York: John Wiley & Sons, 1992, p. 184. Reprinted with permission.

*make $30,000 a year or more, before too long you are likely to be
confronting questions like these:*
> *Is a contract to my advantage?*
> *What should it cover?*
> *How long should it run?*
> *What are the dangers?*
> *What happens if I want to break my contract?*
> *How can I negotiate the best possible agreement?*[1]

The Four Ps

In my earlier book, *Finding the Right Job at Midlife*, I presented some
guidelines to follow in developing an employment contract. I call them the
Four Ps:

- Person
- Proper timing
- Presentation
- Policy[2]

Person. Be sure that you are dealing with a decision maker when negotiating an employment agreement. Talk to someone who has actual hiring
authority, not a personnel administrator.

Proper Timing. From my experience, about 80 percent of all employment
agreements are negotiated before a person reports to work, but they are
rarely, if ever, negotiated during the first interview.

Generally speaking, if you are called back for a second interview, you
will be made an offer 60 percent of the time. If you are offered a job, this
is the time to discuss an employment contract.

Presentation. Once you are offered the job, everyone is going to feel good.
This is the time to suggest that a short agreement be prepared outlining
the terms of the offer. The interviewer might flinch at this, but you can ease
the tension by offering to prepare it yourself: "It's simply a memorandum
of understanding. I can draft one tonight and drop it off tomorrow for you

---

[1] John Tarrant, *Perks and Parachutes* (New York: Simon & Schuster, 1986).

[2] Jeffrey G. Allen, *Finding the Right Job at Midlife* (New York: John Wiley & Sons,
1985).

to look at." Keep your tone positive and upbeat. Don't make it sound as though you will be running to a lawyer to hog-tie the company.

Policy. If the employer decides to let you prepare the memorandum of understanding, whatever you do, don't title it an "Employment Contract." This will raise a red flag. Everything will grind to a halt, and they will eventually begin considering other candidates.

Some suggested language for a basic employment contract is presented in the side bar. Read the explanations after each paragraph to make sure you understand how and why to incorporate these points. Note that the document is called a "Memorandum of Agreement."

Second Thoughts

If you're about to accept a job from an employer who has no written policies and will sign no written agreement, you'd be wise to rethink your decision. Beware of any verbal offer that sounds too good to be true. Go for something that may sound less exciting but feels more solid.

IN THE INTERIM

Get a Reference Letter

As I noted in *The Perfect Job Reference*:

> *The time to get a reference letter from a supervisor is before your coworkers cut your cake. This letter will come in handy in the future if your supervisor runs away from home, goes crazy, dies, or tries to block your career path.*[3]

Before you ask for a reference letter, review your accomplishments in the position you are leaving and offer to prepare a draft for the person to review.

Take a Breather

Try to take a little time off before you start the new job, but use it wisely.

First, you can use the time to get your support system in place. Have you worked out your transportation arrangements? Child care? Will you need a job coach or other on-the-job assistance from anyone? Do you need clothes for the job? Take care of all these behind-the-scenes details before you report to work.

---

[3] Jeffrey G. Allen, *The Perfect Job Reference* (New York: John Wiley & Sons, 1990).

MEMORANDUM OF AGREEMENT

In consideration of __(name of employer)__ hiring __(full name of employee)__, it is agreed as follows:

[Typical Paragraph]

The employee shall be paid a total of $ _____
per _____, less any customary and usual
deductions for the performance of services in the initial position
of _____. Said total amount shall be
increased by at least _____ percent per
year on or before the anniversary date of employment. Changes
in title or responsibilities shall be at the sole discretion of the
employer.

This paragraph discusses an important issue—money. Leave the
percentage blank to give the supervisor a chance to negotiate a figure.
No one likes to be told how much of a raise to give you, but by putting
the blank in for agreement, you have put the subject on the table for
discussion.

[Typical Paragraph]

If employer terminates the employee after 90 days for any
reason other than a specific violation of a written policy
formerly acknowledged by the employee,
_____ times the current weekly gross
amount shall be immediately paid to employee. Said amount
includes pay in place of notice and severance pay, but excludes
any personal leave, sick leave, holiday, vacation, or other pro
rata termination pay in accordance with company policy.

The severance clause spells out what benefits—including out-
placement services—you will receive if, through no fault of your own,
you are fired or laid off. To determine a reasonable severance pay
figure, make a quick call to the personnel department (but don't let
them know you are drafting an employment agreement). When you
have the number, double it. For reference, four weeks is usually the
most a newly hired person can receive.

[Typical Paragraph]

Employee acknowledges that the internal procedures, lists,
records, forms, and other proprietary information developed or
obtained by employer while conducting business are
confidential trade secrets and shall remain the sole property of
employer. Accordingly, employee shall not retain, duplicate,

disclose, or make use of any said proprietary information except as required by the specifications of employment.

By emphasizing your professional responsibility, this paragraph can help you avoid liability for unfair competition if you leave the company.

[Typical Paragraph]

Employee agrees to act in an attentive, ethical, and responsible manner, and to represent exclusively the employer at all times with the utmost concern for its goals, interest, and image with its employees, customers, suppliers, and all others with whom they come in contact during the conduct of business.

This is known as the "best efforts" paragraph. Some form of this wording is found in most employment agreements. It is a way to counterbalance some of the items you want.

[Typical Paragraph]

If it becomes necessary for employee or employer to enforce or interpret the terms of this agreement, matters will be resolved by binding arbitration under the auspices and in accordance with the rules of the American Arbitration Association. Any judgment on the decision rendered may be entered in any court of competent jurisdiction.

This is an important point to mention because the company hiring you can better afford to litigate a dispute in the court system than you can. Binding arbitration is a thoroughly professional and much less expensive way to resolve disputes.

[Typical Paragraph]

Neither employee nor employer shall disclose either the existence of this agreement or any of its terms for the duration of said employment. If employee directly or indirectly causes such disclosure, employer may immediately terminate the employment, as though a written policy formerly acknowledged by employee had been violated.

Your willingness to respect the confidentiality of the agreement is one of the most powerful arguments you have to get it signed quickly.

You can also use the time to organize and prune all your job-hunting notes and files. Store them in an accessible place so that you won't have to start from scratch the next time you're looking for a job.

Tie up personal loose ends. Contact everyone who greased the wheels of your job search. A phone call, a sincere letter, or a thoughtful gift will let them know you appreciated their support and keep your net working for you.

Finally, write to any employers who may still be considering you as a candidate to thank them for their time and consideration. Let them know you have accepted another job, but don't slam any doors. These could be potential employers the next time around. Express hope that you will have an opportunity to work together in the future.

Resign with Refinement

Don't burn any bridges. Give proper notice, help in the hiring or training of your replacement, and clear out your work space.

Begin Again

It's your first day on the new job. But some day—one hopes not too soon—you're going to want to move up, on, or out. Keep track of your accomplishments in the new job so that when it's time to write a resume you'll be ready. Keep your contacts alive and your options open. Although your job is a priority in the near term, your *career* is even more important in the long run.

SITUATION ANALYSES

Situation No. 1

Robert K. is a paraplegic and the sole means of support for his family. As an aircraft systems analyst, he knows that "job security" is a contradiction in terms. He has been invited back for a second interview at a large company and has prepared an employment agreement as a type of "disability insurance policy." The interviewer doesn't know about it.

Robert has already been recommended by the first interviewer and will now meet with the hiring supervisor. An offer is likely to be extended.

Should he call the interviewer and mention the employment agreement? Should he wait and mention it personally to the supervisor? Should he wait until the offer is extended? Can he use the ADA to bind the employer to the job offer before he presents the agreement?

Analysis. I wouldn't advise Robert to call the interviewer about the employment agreement. The only reason for calling would be to avoid the element of surprise. Weighed against the probability that he would short-circuit the interviewing process, waiting is better.

The supervisor is more likely to accept the idea of an agreement because he's not as close to company administration as the interviewer is.

In fact, many supervisors actively assist applicants in getting employment agreements signed.

Waiting until the offer is extended is the best strategy. At that point, the decision to hire has been made and Robert has the most leverage.

This is not an ADA issue. Even the retaliation provisions don't apply because Robert will apparently be hired unless the agreement interferes with the process.

Situation No. 2

Marla B. is a security guard who has a severe knee pain that will require surgery unless she finds a sedentary job.

She has interviewed for an office job with her current employer. It looks like an offer will be extended, but because of Marla's lack of experience on the new job, the pay is 10 percent less than she is making now.

Marla believes that she is being discriminated against because she will be disabled if she stays in her former job. When she expresses her point of view, the human resources manager threatens her with termination unless she accepts the transfer. Marla is now concerned that even if she transfers at the lower pay, the employer will fire her shortly. Does the ADA protect her?

Analysis. Marla is protected from being fired if she accepts the reassignment. Even if she was abusive in what she said, the employer probably can't retaliate because the subject was job discrimination. The law recognizes a clear privilege for employees and others to prevent or correct discriminatory practices.

The employer is within its rights to lower Marla's pay in the desk job based on her inexperience. However, the rate of pay must be comparable to others with equivalent qualifications.

The ADA balances equal employment opportunity with business necessity. It is a flexible law that often encourages compliance.

Marla's case is an example of how it does so.

Situation No. 3

Matthew F. is a blind computer whiz. He is strongly independent and insists on moving about without assistance. He doesn't even own a cane.

On his fourth interview with a major computer manufacturer, he accepts a great offer from the supervisor. He's the best applicant by far, and the firm would pay a lot to get him.

After accepting the offer, Matthew is escorted to the human resources department to meet the interviewer. He falls, stumbles over to the interviewer's chair, and sits behind the desk. This prompts the interviewer to insist that he use a cane on the job. Matthew refuses in no uncertain terms. Must he be hired? Must he use a cane on the job? Does the employer have to buy it? What if Matthew wants a $7,500 experimental radar-sonar-computer-enhanced walking stick?

Analysis. Matthew doesn't have an absolute right to the job.

His use of a cane at work is more than a matter of personal preference—it is a safety issue. It may not be necessary to perform an "essential function" of the job, but getting to work safely is also a legitimate employer concern.

The employer can require any reasonable precaution to protect employees on the premises. Canes are inexpensive, and they greatly reduce slip-and-fall risks for people with vision problems. Matthew's refusal to use one could cost him the job.

If he doesn't buy the cane, the employer would be liable for it. But a radar-sonar-computer-enhanced walking stick? Hardly. Maybe Matthew will earn it as "employee of the year."

CHAPTER ELEVEN

Interview Questions and Answers

TOP 20 INTERVIEW QUESTIONS

Career Path Questions

Why are you leaving your present job?
I'd like to take on more responsibility and learn more about the area of _____. The potential in my present position is limited because of __(the size of the company, the company's emphasis on other areas, limited product line, etc.)__.

What do you expect to be doing in five years?
Five years from now, I see myself working for this company. My job will have increased at least one, probably two levels in responsibility and scope. I'll have made a significant contribution to the _____ department and will be working on new ways to _____ _____. Ten years from now, I will have progressed up the ladder into management by proving that I'm a producer and a problem solver.

What are your long-term career goals?
[First give specifics about your profession and what level you hope to attain within it:]

I have given my career a great deal of thought in recent months, and in the process I've mapped out a plan for achieving my long-term goals. This position is an important step in that plan.

Why did you change jobs so often?
[Your answer should explain the reason, then emphasize your future plans for more stability:]

Early in my career I made a few job changes at relatively short intervals. In one case, I accepted an entry-level position on the basis that I would be promoted within six months. After a year of working below my capacity, I realized I needed to move out in order to move up.

In another situation, my department was reorganized right after I was hired, and I was moved into a different position that didn't suit my background as well. I tried to make it work for six months, but it was an obvious mismatch. I did a good job, but I just wasn't happy.

In a third instance, my division was purchased by _____ _____ and the plant was closed.

These experiences have taught me to select my jobs carefully and to chart a definite course for my career. I'm looking now for an employer committed to building a long-term working relationship with me—one that will be to our mutual benefit.

Why do you want this job?
I'm interested in this job because it appears to offer exactly what I'm looking for, both in terms of the position itself and the overall environment of the company. My career goal is to _____, and I think this job would allow me to develop my potential in that direction.

My experience in _____ and my training in _____ have equipped me to perform the job you need done. After studying the history and future plans of the company, meeting people who work here, and seeing the kinds of jobs there are to be done, it seems like a perfect fit.

Background and Character Questions

Tell me about yourself.
[Prepare a one-minute response that includes your name, geographic ties, referrals, experience, skills, major character traits, and work values. Depending upon your disclosure strategy, you might find this to be a natural place to mention your disability as it relates to your work.]

My name is _____. I was born in Chicago and have lived here all my life. I was educated at local public schools and earned my bachelor's degree in geology at the University of Illinois. I've been with the Environmental Sciences Laboratory for three years now, analyzing water and soil samples for about 15 major corporate clients. I value excellence in my work. The state-of-the-art equipment you use in your facility, which I read about in *Business Week* a few months ago, would give me a chance to carry my analyses to the next level—and beyond.

In terms of my work style, I'm a self-starter, energetic and results oriented. I'm also a good team player because my enthusiasm is contagious. I can generally motivate people around me to focus on a goal and attain it. As a result, the groups I've worked with have been highly charged and very successful.

[Optional disclosure:] When I lost my leg in a car accident five years ago, my energy and enthusiasm were put to the test, but I was back on the job within a matter of weeks.

What is your main strength?

My main strength is probably my desire to honor my commitments. I take great pride in delivering on my promises—on the job and in my personal life. I'm also able to get along with people, regardless of their backgrounds or personalities.

What is your main weakness?

[Never pick a real weakness, or one that's related to your disability. Choose one that's trivial or is actually a strength.]

I tend to be preoccupied with doing my job. Some people consider that to be one of my strengths.

What specific strengths would you bring to this position?

My education in _____, my experience in _____, and my knowledge of _____ will enable me to step into this position with little or no downtime. Because I know how to transfer my skills from one job to another, I can learn my way around an organization quickly. That means I can concentrate on developing solid working relationships.

What do you do when you have trouble solving a problem?

One thing I don't do is ignore it. I'm not afraid to ask questions or look for answers myself. I'm a problem solver by nature, so when something puzzles me I keep at it until I find a solution. Sometimes it just takes creative investigation.

Before I act, though, I think. I try to distance myself from the problem so that I can look at it objectively. Sometimes I write it down or diagram it to see it more clearly.

Work Style Questions

Do you prefer working as a member of a team, or would you rather work alone?

Working as part of a team is one of the most important elements in a successful career. If you can't work well in a team, you probably can't function well one-on-one either.

On the other hand, I can work just as hard alone. Whether I prefer to work as part of a team or individually depends on the task at hand. Either way, I work equally hard with the initiative required for success.

Do you like to work with people?

Without a doubt. If we're to meet our goals and keep up with the growth that's predicted for this industry, we'll have to organize and coordinate the efforts of many people. There's a synergy in teamwork that can accomplish far more than the same individuals could working alone. When a group of people is working together, there's nothing like it. The energy and creativity we activate in each other are many times greater.

[If the job requires solitary hours analyzing reports or crunching numbers:]

I've always worked well with others, but I have no difficulty getting my work done independently. I'm a self-starter—I can set my own goals or take assigned goals and complete them. I'm comfortable with myself.

How do you react to criticism from superiors, if you believe it is unwarranted?

Criticism is never unwarranted, but it's often *unwelcome*. Even unnecessary criticism is caused by something. If it was something I did, I want to know. I've found that if I think before I react, I can view a person's comments more objectively—as feedback to my *actions*, not a rejection of *me*.

Do you work well under pressure?

I've developed several coping techniques. For one thing, I eat properly, exercise regularly, and take vitamins. When work causes tension for whatever reason—deadlines, schedules, special projects—I'm ready.

Also, I try to keep a perspective on the situation. My history has proven that there's nothing I can't accomplish if I put my mind to it. I try to turn mountains into stepping stones. I realize that no stressful situation lasts forever, so I set my sights high and keep climbing without looking down.

Are you able to work alone without direct supervision?

Definitely. I'm a self-starter *and* finisher. I usually need direction only once—the first time I do something. From then on, I work well on my own. I enjoy applying my creativity and problem-solving skills to my work.

On the other hand, I'm not afraid to ask questions. If I'm not sure about a task or the expected results, I check with the person in charge. The important thing is to get the job done right.

What three areas of your job do you like the least?

I really like this work, so I can't think of any major dislikes. I guess my answers would come under the category of "annoyances."

The biggest annoyance is people who don't care about the company's goals—people who are just "putting in their time." It happens everywhere you work, but I can't help thinking that if everyone would concentrate on the business at hand, we'd all accomplish even more.

Then there's the usual paperwork that seems to slow down the action. I realize the importance of documentation, and I always fill out the required forms and time logs, but I'm always looking for efficiencies in that area so I can get back to my job. I'd rather be on top of my paperwork than the other way around.

Availability Questions

Are you able to work overtime if necessary?
Yes, as long as I have some advance notice. A job is a lot more than a paycheck—it's a responsibility. When I am given the responsibility for a job, I take it seriously. I make sure it gets done, even if it means working late. Whether I'm compensated for overtime or not, I derive personal satisfaction from the extra effort that results in success.

Do you have a good work attendance record?
[If your work record shows extended absence as the result of an injury or illness that is no longer a factor, explain what happened and why it no longer affects your attendance. Otherwise use the following:]

No. My attendance record is very good. I'm in good health and rebound quickly. I think you'll see when you check that the few days I missed work were due to the usual flu viruses going around. I figure that when you're sick it's better to take one day off and get well rather than going to the office, working at half speed, and taking more time off to recuperate. I'd rather work at home when I'm sick than expose coworkers to my illness.

May we contact your present employer?
No. I've decided not to tell my employer I'm changing jobs until there's a firm offer on the table. My boss deserves the courtesy of hearing the news from me. He (She) will be disappointed, but I'll do everything I can to ensure a smooth transition. You'll probably get more than a reference— you might get a testimonial.

[If your employer knows you are interviewing and would give you a good reference:]

Yes. My employer knows that I'm interviewing and understands why. He (She) is very happy with the work I've been doing, but the company has no position available that would allow me to develop in my career. I've trained my staff well over the past _____ years. They deserve a chance to move up, and I need to use more of my potential. I'll always value the experience I gained there and will use what I learned throughout my career.

Please let me know before you call so I can let him (her) down gently.

Do you have any questions?
[This is not the time to inquire about salary and benefits. Questions relating to the structure of the company, duties of the position, or nature of the product line would all be appropriate here. Make sure you're comfortable with your topic before asking the question. For example:]

Yes. You mentioned you'd be expanding your Albuquerque packaging plant, which would create about a hundred new positions. Do you have any other expansion plans?

[Or:]

Yes, I have a question regarding the organization of the department. You mentioned that this position reports to the director of customer service but also falls within the authority of the marketing department. Is there also a director of marketing to whom I would report? If so, where does the company divide the responsibilities of each director?

[Don't ask a question just for appearances' sake. If it was a lengthy interview and all of your questions have been covered, it is perfectly all right to say:]

I had many questions, but you've answered them all. You've been very helpful, and I'm more excited than ever about this opportunity.

COMMON DISABILITY-RELATED QUESTIONS

In addition to the standard questions, the interviewer might raise some disability-related issues, either directly or indirectly. Most of the concerns rest on unfounded stereotypes about workers with disabilities. Arm yourself with the statistics you need to blow these myths out of the water. Consult two recent Harris surveys: *Public Attitudes Toward People with Disabilities* (1991), conducted for the National Organization on Disability ($25), and *Employing Disabled Americans* (1986), conducted for the International Center for the Disabled ($20).

I can't envision how you would do this job. Could you give me a demonstration?
This is a perfectly legitimate question under the ADA, and one that you'll have to be prepared to address if you really want the job. You can convince the interviewer that your disability will not stand in your way by bringing your tools and adaptive equipment with you and demonstrating how they are used. Careers journalist Melanie Witt also advises giving the interviewer the names and phone numbers of a few successfully employed people with similar disabilities or the names of employers who have hired people in

your circumstances. You will, of course, have to contact all of them in advance to enlist their support.

What happens if you're injured on the job?
There is no evidence to support the notion that workers with disabilities are more injury- or accident-prone than other workers. In fact, nearly half of the employers surveyed in the 1986 Harris poll agreed that workers with disabilities have *fewer* accidents on the job than workers without disabilities. Cite your own work record in support of these findings. In any event, under the ADA, an employer cannot ask you about your worker's compensation history, nor do you have to prove that you won't present a significant health or safety risk to yourself or others.

Will you be able to evacuate the building in an emergency?
Explain the buddy system—two or three employees who volunteer to help you exit the building safely. If you use a wheelchair, describe how your "buddies" would carry you down the stairs.

Will my insurance rates go up if I hire you?
This fear is based on the false assumption that people with disabilities file more health and injury claims. In reality, their rates are comparable to those of other employees. In any event, group insurance rates are determined by a company's overall experience, not by the physical characteristics of individual employees covered by the group plan. In some cases, the claims are spread over a large pool of employees from *several* organizations.

Do you think you'll fit in with the rest of the staff?
Although most people still feel uncomfortable in the presence of a person with a disability, a massive 93 percent of the employers participating in the 1986 Harris poll rejected the argument that disabled employees don't fit in. Share these findings with the interviewer, and assure him or her that you will assume responsibility for making those around you feel more at ease with your disability. Avoid letting third parties, such as personnel managers, convey their impressions of you. You want the chance to evaluate the potential success of your working relationships firsthand.

Does your disability interfere with your attendance?
This concern stems from the traditional view of blindness and other forms of disability as "sicknesses." As a result, many employers fear that workers with disabilities may be sick more often. There is no evidence to support such fears. In fact, surveys show just the opposite: disabled workers have unusually good attendance records.

This is a pretty fast-paced environment. Are you sure you'll be able to keep up?
Both the 1986 and the 1991 Harris surveys indicate that workers with

disabilities are as productive or *more productive* than other workers. Assure the employer that you expect to be held to the same standards of quality and productivity as everyone else.

Our corporate profits are down for the year. How can I afford to provide you with expensive adaptive equipment?
The real challenge of accommodation is one of creativity. According to the database listings of the Job Accommodation Network, a project of the President's Committee on the Employment of People with Disabilities, the average cost of an accommodation is $32, and about a third of the accommodations provided cost nothing. There are also tax credits and other monetary incentives for employers who hire people with disabilities and provide accommodations to them (see Chapter 12). Be prepared to discuss these resources with the interviewer.

In some cases, the employer might ask you to share the cost of an accommodation. Your willingness to do so will be viewed as evidence of your desire to be an equal contributor to the organization. If you cannot afford to shoulder any of the costs yourself, arrange for a third party, such as a rehabilitation agency, to pay for your share. Once you prove yourself as a hard-working member of the department, your employer will probably be more than willing to spend money to increase your productivity and to make your work more convenient.

What if the whole building has to be retrofitted to accommodate you?
Employers worry that they will have to undertake major structural changes in the building to install braille signage throughout a building, reconfigure their offices, or build separate lunchroom facilities to accommodate a worker with disabilities. This is a much larger issue—it has nothing to do with your job qualifications.

You can respond first with an upbeat statement: "The fact that I'm sitting here with you now speaks well of your facility." But having said this, quickly point out that you are not an architect and so are not qualified to discuss whether or not the building conforms to federally mandated accessibility standards. If the employer rents the space, this is an issue for the building owner or manager. Be helpful in pointing out that copies of the accessibility guidelines are available from the Architectural and Transportation Barriers Compliance Board (800/USA-ABLE or 202/272-5434), which also sponsors a technical assistance hotline. Many other trade associations, government agencies, and disability groups provide free or low-cost consulting services.

Your objective is to focus on accommodations that are related to your particular job.

How much assistance do you think you'll require from your coworkers?

To dispel the myth of dependency, you need to expand the employer's thinking about your capabilities. Offer examples of situations in which you used your native intelligence or your physical strength. Draw upon work experiences, community involvement, or leisure activities that show you in a supportive, giving role.

You might also want to discuss job restructuring strategies that would allow you to perform your job with little or no assistance from your coworkers (see Chapter 12).

Finally, keep in mind that in the modern workplace, where the emphasis is on teamwork and cooperation, no one is totally independent.

What happens if you don't work out on the job?

You may not be asked this directly, but it is an underlying concern for employers. Try to approach the issue by making a case for why you think you *will* work out. In the 1986 Harris poll, 88 percent of top managers gave employees with disabilities an "excellent" or "good" rating on key job criteria such as reliability, attendance, and productivity. Cite these and other facts documenting the productivity of workers with disabilities to build a case for your candidacy.

When it comes down to firing, though, managers are uneasy about having to lower the boom on someone with a disability. Forty-four percent of the managers in the 1986 Harris survey said it is more difficult to fire someone with a disability than it is to fire a nondisabled worker. That perception is a barrier to your employment, but you can scale it with a strong, positive statement such as, "I'm sure I wouldn't have any trouble meeting your company's high standards, but if I didn't I would expect to be released."

My staff is not trained to work with disabled people.

An overwhelming majority (82 percent) of line managers participating in the 1986 Harris survey indicated that disabled employees are no more difficult to supervise than others. Knowing this, you might say something like: "Working with disabled people is essentially the same as working with any group of people. We want what anyone wants: We want to show what we can accomplish; we want performance appraisals based on facts; and we want control over our lives to the extent possible."

SITUATION ANALYSES

Situation No. 1

Ruth T. has a nerve disorder but has adjusted to it in her job as a hotel manager. Over the past month, she has taken almost three weeks off to undergo neurological treatment.

She also used the time to interview with a competing hotel and has been invited back for a second interview. Unfortunately, her boss took the message. He wrote an "urgent" note with it requesting to meet with her.

The competitor knows about Ruth's illness but doesn't care. Its insurance program provides limited coverage for her disorder. She wants to stay with her present employer but is afraid that this meeting with her boss will be her last.

Can the ADA be used to keep Ruth working at her present job with full insurance benefits? If not, can she at least require the present group insurance carrier to continue covering her? Can the ADA be used to require the prospective employer's insurance carrier to give her the same coverage for the disability as the former one?

Analysis. Ruth had better play hardball fast. She should go to the closest Equal Employment Opportunity Commission (EEOC) office and file a discrimination charge.

The ADA is "protective labor law." This means she can't be fired until disposition of the charge. There are also protections against retaliation for filing such charges.

The ADA doesn't specifically require the present insurance carrier to continue coverage. It also doesn't require the prospective employer's insurance carrier to issue anything beyond its standard group coverage.

Situation No. 2

Henry C. is a hearing-impaired waiter who is often accused of having eyes in the back of his head. He's the best, but he changes jobs every six months or so.

Henry applies for a job with one of the finest restaurants in town. At the second interview, the owner expresses concern that Henry will be unable to hear customers and coworkers.

A computerized menu-ordering system would help Henry on the job, but it would cost more than he earned in a month. The owner also fears that it would detract from the restaurant's ambience.

Henry is happy just "doing his thing" as the world's best waiter, but he has already made an appointment with the EEOC.

If Henry is not hired, will the EEOC consultant investigate the charge? What will the outcome be?

Analysis. The owner's concern about the restaurant's image doesn't appear to be reasonable.

Henry is an experienced waiter and should be given the opportunity to do the job. If he declined to wear the waiters' uniform or otherwise refused to comply with accepted restaurant policies, there would be no obligation to hire him.

The computerized ordering system appears to be an undue hardship on the owner. However, he can't require it himself solely to prevent Henry from being hired. Objectively, it appears unnecessary.

So Henry should file the charge. The owner will be required to hire him. Given his work history, he's probably just passin' through anyway.

CHAPTER TWELVE

Reasonable Accommodations under Title I

The reasonable accommodations requirement of the Americans with Disabilities Act (ADA) is meant to remove employment barriers for people with disabilities. These barriers may be structural obstacles that inhibit access to job sites or equipment; they may be rigid work schedules that dictate when work is performed; or they may be inflexible job procedures that limit the modes of communication that are used on the job or the way in which particular tasks are accomplished.

Under Title I of the ADA, employers are obligated to provide accommodations in three broad areas:

- Accommodations that provide equal opportunity in the job application process.
- Accommodations that enable workers on the job to perform the essential functions of a position.
- Accommodations that allow people with disabilities to enjoy all the benefits and privileges of employment—cafeterias, lounges, auditoriums, transportation, counseling, training, and other employer-sponsored services or programs.

An individual's need for an accommodation in any of these areas cannot enter into decisions regarding hiring, firing, or promotion unless the accommodation would impose an undue hardship on the business.

WHAT IS AN ACCOMMODATION?

An accommodation is any change in the work environment or in the way things are usually done. There is nothing new or mysterious about accommodations—they are made every day to help workers with and without disabilities do a better job. One person might need a brighter light; another might need a stepstool or a nonglare computer screen.

As defined in the ADA, accommodation entails:

1.   Making existing facilities readily accessible to and usable by individuals with disabilities. These are *structural accommodations* and will be discussed in the following chapter.

2.   Restructuring jobs; modifying work schedules; reassigning workers with disabilities to vacant positions; modifying examinations, training materials, or policies; acquiring or modifying equipment; providing qualified readers or interpreters. These are *operational and equipment-related accommodations*, many of which cost little or nothing to implement. We'll explore these options in more detail in this chapter.

OPERATIONAL ACCOMMODATIONS

Job Restructuring

The key to job restructuring is flexibility. While essential functions need not be eliminated, nonessential elements can be assigned to another employee. If essential duties cannot be performed or reassigned, an applicant with a disability need not be hired.

Example _____

> Suppose a security guard position requires the individual to inspect identification cards. An employer would not have to provide someone who is blind with an assistant to look at the cards because, in this situation, the assistant would be *performing* the job rather than *helping* with it.

A job can also be restructured by altering when and how an essential function is performed. For example, an essential function that is usually performed in the early morning might be rescheduled until later in the day. Someone who has trouble writing might be permitted to computerize records that were previously maintained manually.

Typical Job-Restructuring Accommodations

- *Job rotation.* A worker with limited strength or endurance for a spe-

cific job task can rotate to an alternate job that does not require the same physical exertion.
*   ***Sequencing.*** An assembly worker with a learning disability can assemble the product when the pieces are presented in a set sequence. Parts can be organized in numbered boxes.
*   ***Job expansion.*** A VDT operator with a cumulative trauma disorder can do the support work (filing, copying, phone) for one manager rather than VDT data entry for four managers.

Modified Work Schedules

Some people with disabilities require modified work schedules because they need regular medical treatment or because they must depend on transportation that limits their hours of travel. While the ADA does not demand that employers abandon all attendance and punctuality rules, those rules must be applied carefully and with an understanding of the law. The employer doesn't have to provide additional *paid* sick leave to disabled workers but may have to provide additional *unpaid* leave as a reasonable accommodation.

Example

A worker recovering from cancer needs one day off a week for chemotherapy. A four-day workweek, 10 hours per day, would accommodate this.

Reassignment

The reassignment option is available only to people who are on the job, not to job applicants. When a worker on the job requests a reassignment due to a disability, the employer may not force that person into an undesirable position or segregate him or her into a designated office. The individual must be reassigned to an equivalent position in terms of pay and status, if he or she is qualified and if the position is vacant within a reasonable amount of time.

An individual can be reassigned to a lower-graded position if there are no accommodations that would enable the employee to remain in the current position and there are no vacant equivalent positions for which he or she is qualified. An employer is *not* required to maintain the reassigned individual at the salary of the higher-graded position or to promote someone with a disability to a higher-graded position for which he or she is not qualified.

In either case, remember that you can only be reassigned to a *vacant* position. *Another employee need not be bumped out of a position to accommodate your disability.*

Even bona fide seniority systems can be challenged under the ADA, but the law doesn't specify just how a unionized employer should balance its ADA obligations against commitments imposed by a union contract or collective bargaining agreement.

For example, it is not clear that an employer may reassign an employee with a disability to a vacant position if a labor contract reserves certain jobs for employees with a given amount of seniority. If an employer decides to award a vacant job to an employee with a disability, it may be financially liable to a more senior worker for violating his or her rights under the labor contract.

Modification of Examinations, Training Materials, or Policies

To give all qualified applicants an equal opportunity to compete for a position, the ADA requires that an employer provide, upon advance request, alternative, accessible tests to individuals with disabilities that impair the sensory, manual, or speaking skills needed to take the test—unless the tests are specifically intended to measure those functions. That means an employer might have to administer a preemployment test orally instead of in writing, or in large print or braille, or by means of a reader or sign interpreter. In some cases, a person might have to be allowed more time for a test. Where it is not possible to test in an alternative format, the employer may be required as a reasonable accommodation to evaluate the skill to be tested in another manner (e.g., through an interview or through work experience requirements). The obligation to make reasonable accommodation in the application process extends to ensuring that the test or interview site itself is accessible.

In terms of policy, the ADA requires an employer to modify any companywide requirement that discriminates against workers with disabilities. A policy requiring all employees to hold a driver's license, for instance, must be modified when applied to a person with a disability who can perform the essential functions of the job but cannot drive. Of course, if driving is an essential function of the job, a license may be required.

Modification of Equipment

Under the ADA, an employer must provide special or modified equipment as a reasonable accommodation to disabled employees or applicants. This includes:

- Electronic visual aids
- Braille materials

- Talking calculators
- Magnifiers
- Audio recordings
- Telephone handset amplifiers
- Telecommunications devices for the deaf
- Mechanical page turners
- Raised or lowered furniture

This obligation extends only to modifications that help a person perform a particular job. It does *not* extend to items that are primarily for personal use outside of the job, such as prosthetic limbs, hearing aids, eyeglasses, wheelchairs, or guide dogs.

Example

> If you have a visual impairment, your employer might have to supply you with special glasses that enable you to use the office computer monitors, as long as those glasses are not needed for your personal use outside of the office.

Readers or Interpreters

Although an employer might have to hire a reader or interpreter to assist someone on the job, the employer need not hire two people to do one job. If an interpreter or reader is required on only a part-time basis and the person may perform other work for the employer, his or her services may be reasonable. Because readers and interpreters are among the most expensive of the accommodations required by the ADA, the key to assessing whether they must be provided is the concept of undue hardship, which is discussed later in this chapter.

Other Accommodations

In addition to the specific reasonable accommodations listed in the ADA itself, the interpretive guidelines of the Equal Employment Opportunity Commission (EEOC) suggest the following:

- Permitting the use of accrued paid leave or providing additional unpaid leave for necessary treatment.
- Providing reserved parking spaces.
- Making employer-provided transportation accessible.
- Providing personal assistants such as page turners or travel attendants.
- Providing temporary job coaches to assist in training.

THE ACCOMMODATION PROCESS

Who Initiates Process?

Generally, you—the employee or job applicant—are responsible for requesting an accommodation. However, if you have a known disability and are having difficulty performing on the job, the employer can ask if you need an accommodation. A small, independently owned business might not have a formal procedure for requesting accommodations, but a larger company should have clear-cut written procedures. They ought to be posted in lunchrooms, copier rooms, and coffee stations. As explained in Chapter 8, a request for an accommodation goes hand in hand with disclosure.

How to Begin

1. Make your request in writing.
2. Have medical records to document the nature or extent of your disability.
3. Know what you need and what it will cost.
4. Keep copies of all requests and responses on file.

Choosing an Accommodation: A Problem-Solving Approach

The EEOC's regulations describe the reasonable accommodation process as a "problem-solving approach" that directly involves the employee in attempting to fashion an appropriate solution. A person usually knows exactly what he or she needs to do a job, and this accommodation might be simpler and less expensive than one devised by the employer acting alone. So it makes sense to work together to identify particular tasks that limit performance.[1]

A four-step process can be used to arrive at a mutually satisfactory accommodation:

1. Identify barriers to performance. Pinpoint for the employer how the impairment limits your ability to fulfill specific job tasks. Take into account both essential and nonessential functions.
2. Work together to identify all possible accommodations; get outside help if necessary. Here, too, you probably have more experience and insight than the employer, so take the lead and try to be helpful. Know about

---

[1] Zachary Fasman, *What Business Must Know About the ADA: 1992 Compliance Guide* (Washington, DC: U.S. Chamber of Commerce, 1992), 22.

tax incentives (discussed later in this chapter), funding, and sources of technical assistance.

3. *Assess the reasonableness of each accommodation.* Make sure you are aware of the employer's legal defenses, including undue hardship and threats to health or safety. These are discussed later in this chapter.

4. *Try to agree upon an appropriate accommodation.* The accommodations that work best are those that benefit both the employee *and* the company.

Reasonable versus Best: Who Decides?

The employer has the final say in selecting an accommodation. EEOC regulations state that if two suggested accommodations would work equally well, the employer can choose the one that is less expensive or easier to implement. An accommodation must be adequate to enable the person to perform the essential functions of the job, but it does not have to be the "best" accommodation possible.

If you are not happy with the employer's solution, you might suggest implementing your preferred accommodation on a trial basis, reserving the right to insist upon another method if it disrupts the workplace or harms you or your coworkers.

Who Pays?

The answer to this question hinges on the notion of *undue hardship*, discussed later in the chapter. An employer that can afford to pay for a reasonable accommodation is obliged to do so. If the employer cannot afford to provide the requested accommodation, you—the job applicant or employee—must be given the opportunity to pay for a portion of it. Your willingness to share costs and your initiative in finding outside funding sources could land you the job.

Depending upon how much you want the job, you might consider taking out a loan from a bank or credit union to finance your portion of the accommodation. Another source is CATS (Computer-Assisted Technology Services), a program of the National Easter Seal Society. CATS is a national loan fund to help people with disabilities purchase employment-related adaptive technologies.

REASONABLE ACCOMMODATION PROCESS ILLUSTRATED

The following example illustrates the four-step process outlined above.

Suppose a sack-handler position requires that the employee pick up 50-pound sacks and carry them from the loading dock to the storage room, and that a sack handler who is disabled by a back impairment requests a reasonable accommodation. Upon receiving the request, the employer analyzes the position and determines that its essential function and purpose is not to physically lift and carry the sacks but to transport them from the loading dock to the storage room.

The employer then meets with the sack handler to find out just how his disability limits his performance of the job's essential function of transporting the sacks. At this meeting the employer learns that the individual can lift the sacks to waist level but cannot carry them from the loading dock to the storage room. The employer and the individual agree that any of a number of accommodations, such as a dolly, hand truck, or cart, could enable the sack handler to transport the sacks.

Upon further consideration, it is determined that a cart is not a feasible option. No carts are currently available at the company, and those that can be purchased are the wrong shape to hold many of the bulky and irregularly shaped sacks that must be moved. Both the dolly and the hand truck, on the other hand, appear to be effective options, and both are readily available.

The employee indicates his preference for the dolly. In consideration of this preference, and because the employer feels that the dolly will allow the man to move more sacks at a time than would a hand truck, the employer provides the sack handler with a dolly in fulfillment of the obligation to make reasonable accommodation.

What Constitutes Failure to Make Reasonable Accommodation?

To establish that an employer unlawfully failed to provide a reasonable accommodation, you must show that:

1. You were otherwise qualified for the position.
2. A reasonable accommodation existed that would have enabled you to perform the essential functions of the job.
3. The accommodation was requested but not provided.

EMPLOYER DEFENSES

Health and Safety Risks

An employer doesn't have to hire someone who cannot perform the essential duties of the job without posing a direct threat to his or her own health or safety or that of others. The EEOC will consider the following factors in determining whether the individual poses a direct threat.

- The duration of the risk
- The severity of the risk

- The likelihood that the harm will occur
- The imminence of the harm

Employment decisions must be based on sound medical judgments, not on generalizations, irrational fears, or speculations. For example, fears about emergency evacuations or natural disasters cannot be invoked unless emergency response is an essential part of the job.

Undue Hardship

The test of what's reasonable is made on a case-by-case basis. What may be reasonable for one employer in one situation may be an undue hardship for another in a similar situation. The burden of proof in this matter rests with the employer, but the concept is not precisely defined in the ADA. The law states only that an undue hardship is "an action requiring significant difficulty or expense."

EEOC regulations outline factors to consider in determining an undue hardship:

- The nature and cost of the accommodation, taking into consideration the availability of outside funding and tax credits or deductions. If public funding is available, the employer must investigate and attempt to obtain that funding. Cost thus refers only to the *net* cost of the accommodation.
- The financial resources of the company or facility. If a large company operates several small facilities across the country, the ADA states that the courts should look at local resources as well as the financial resources of the entire enterprise, but it offers no formula for deciding what is more important.
- The impact of the accommodation upon the operation of the company.
- The nature of the business, including the size, composition, and structure of the work force. For example, a nightclub would not be required to accommodate an individual who can perform only in bright lighting if a change in the lighting would destroy the club's ambience or make it difficult to see the show.
- Aggregate accommodation costs. For example, an employer might earmark a certain portion of its earnings for accommodations and spend that amount on a first-come, first-served basis. Several expensive accommodations occurring early in the year might render the employer unable to respond to later requests, even though they may be less costly than those already undertaken.

It is not easy to prove undue hardship. Without documented evidence of specific problems that will be caused by the accommodation—the impact on other employees or the public, the consequences of a loss of efficiency, or the cost in relation to the company's overall budget—an undue hardship claim is difficult to support.[2] Comparing the cost of the accommodation to the salary of the individual is not a proof of undue hardship, nor is the argument of inconvenience.

And remember: Even if an accommodation is too costly, an employer still must offer it as an option and pay its fair share of the cost as long as the employee or applicant is willing to pay for the part that exceeds the undue hardship standard.

COST OF ACCOMMODATION

About 80 percent of top management participating in a 1987 Harris survey conducted for the International Center for the Disabled indicated that accommodating disabled people is *not* expensive. They reported that the average cost of employing a disabled person is about the same as the cost of employing a nondisabled person.

Case in point: Friendly's restaurant in Muncy, Pennsylvania, has employed dozens of people with disabilities over the past several years and has found that most job accommodations were quite simple. One dishwasher using a wheelchair needed a plastic apron to keep dry while sorting silverware. The manager communicated with two deaf employees on a notepad rather than by speaking. In 1986, the manager of the restaurant, Nancy Merrick, received a White House award for her efforts in employing the disabled. "Each person is a different challenge," she says.[3]

The challenge of reasonable accommodation is largely one of creativity. The Friendly's restaurant experience shows that the best solution is not necessarily the most costly. In fact, the database listings of the Job Accommodation Network (JAN) indicate that many accommodations cost less than $100, with an average cost of only $32 (see next section).

Typical Equipment-Related Job Accommodations

The following examples of job accommodations are taken from the JAN database.[4] For more information, call 1-800/JAN-7234.

Modifications of Existing Equipment
* A plant worker who was hearing impaired was able to use a telephone

---

[2]Fasman, *What Business Must Know About the ADA*, 29–30.

[3]Bradford McKee, "Disability Rules Target Job Bias." *Nation's Business*, June 1992.

[4]JAN database. Morgantown, W.Va.: Job Accommodation Network, 1992.

amplifier designed to work in conjunction with hearing aids, allowing him to retain his job. Approximate cost: $25.
•   A receptionist who was blind was provided with a light probe that enabled her to determine which lines on the telephone were ringing, on hold, or in use. Approximate cost: $45.
•   A computer operator with an eye disorder was provided with an anti-glare screen. Approximate cost: $40.
•   A grounds keeper who had recovered from a stroke had limited use of one arm and was unable to rake the grass. A detachable extension arm on the rake allowed him to control the tool with his functional arm. Approximate cost: $20.

New Equipment—Standard
•   A company rented a headset for a phone that allowed an insurance salesperson with cerebral palsy to write while talking on the telephone.
•   An individual with use of only one hand needed to use a camera as part of his job, but a tripod was too cumbersome. By using a waist pod (such as is used to carry flags), he was able to manipulate the camera and keep his job. Approximate cost: $50.
•   A clerk with limited use of her hands was provided with a "lazy Susan" file folder so she would not have to reach across her desk. Approximate cost: $85.
•   A timer with an indicator light allowed a medical technician who was deaf to perform the lab tests required for her job. Approximate cost: $30.
•   A one-handed individual working in a food service position was able to perform all required job tasks except opening cans. Purchase of a one-handed can opener enabled her to perform that remaining task. Approximate cost: $35.
•   A light was installed at the door of a company to alert the security guard to an approaching employee who used a wheelchair and needed assistance with the door. Approximate cost: $50.
•   A police officer with dyslexia had trouble filling out forms at the end of the day. Providing him with a tape recorder and designating a secretary to type out his reports allowed him to continue his job.

Custom Equipment
•   An individual who was short statured was fitted with special seating so that he could drive a heavy loading machine for a construction company.
•   An employee who had worked for 17 years was fitted with a portable air-purifying respirator to alleviate recently acquired allergic reactions to dust and aerosol sprays.
•   A worker with a back injury was supplied with an adjustable-height table to allow for easier manipulation of materials.

• A housekeeper in a motel who had bending restrictions needed to inspect under the beds when she cleaned rooms. A mirror on an extending wand and a reacher allowed her to inspect and reach any items under the bed.

• A radio dispatcher with retinitis pigmentosa (a degenerative eye disease) needed to dial a great many telephone numbers in a hurry. A personal computer with an automatic dialing modem and a voice synthesis system allowed the dispatcher to handle the calls.

• A logger had lost two fingers on his dominant hand. By using a glove with a built-in wrist support, he was able to continue using his chain saw.

• A special chair was provided for a district sales agent who had a back injury.

Zero Cost Solutions
• Turnstiles to the cafeteria were removed to allow people in wheelchairs to enter the facility.

• A person who used a wheelchair could not use the furniture in her office because the desk height was too low for the wheelchair to fit under. Raising the desk with wood blocks allowed extra space for the wheelchair, thus saving the expense of purchasing a special desk.

• The desk layout was changed from the right side to the left for a visually-impaired data entry operator.

• Transferring materials from a vertical filing cabinet into a nearby lateral file enabled a clerk to perform her job from a wheelchair.

TAX INCENTIVES

As mentioned earlier, numerous sources of public funding are available to help businesses comply with the ADA.[5] Be prepared to discuss these with the employer.

Disabled Access Credit

The Disabled Access Credit (DAC) took effect on November 5, 1990, and is now contained in Section 44 of the Internal Revenue Code. This tax incentive is designed to encourage small businesses to comply with the ADA. An eligible small business is one with gross receipts of less than $1 million and fewer than 30 full-time workers.

The DAC credit is equal to 50 percent of all eligible access expenditures

---

[5]*Employees Are Asking About Making the Workplace Accessible to Workers with Disabilities* (Washington, DC: President's Committee on Employment of People with Disabilities, 1991).

of between $250 and $10,250, for a maximum credit of $5,000 a year. In the case of a partnership, the expenditure limit applies to the partnership and to each partner.

Eligible access expenditures include costs incurred for:

- Removing architectural, communications, physical, or transportation barriers that prevent a business from being accessible to, or usable by, individuals with disabilities.
- Providing qualified interpreters or other effective methods of making aurally delivered materials available to individuals with hearing impairments.
- Providing qualified readers, taped texts, and other effective methods of making visually delivered materials available to individuals with visual impairments.
- Acquiring or modifying equipment or devices for individuals with disabilities.
- Providing other similar services, modifications, materials, or equipment.

A small business may deduct the difference between the disabled access credit claimed and the disabled access expenditures incurred, up to $15,000. Disabled access credits can be carried forward up to 15 years and back for 3 years, but not prior to the date of enactment. Expenses incurred for new construction are not eligible.

Architectural and Transportation Barrier Removal Deduction

This provision, contained in Section 190 of the Internal Revenue Code, allows businesses to deduct up to $15,000 for making a facility or public transportation vehicle that is owned or leased for use in the business more accessible to individuals with disabilities. In the case of a partnership, the $15,000 limit applies to the partnership and to each partner.

The deduction may not be used for expenses incurred for new construction, or for a complete renovation of a facility or public transportation vehicle, or for the normal replacement of depreciable property.

For more information on DAC or Section 190 credits, contact a local IRS office or: Office of Chief Counsel, Internal Revenue Service, 1111 Constitution Avenue NW, Washington, DC 20224; 202/566-3292.

Targeted Jobs Tax Credit

The Targeted Jobs Tax Credit (TJTC), contained in Section 51 of the Internal Revenue Code, was established in 1977. It offers employers a credit against their tax liability if they hire individuals from nine targeted groups, which include persons with disabilities. The credit is not available to employers of maids, chauffeurs, or other household employees.

The credit is equal to 40 percent of the first year's wages up to $6,000 per employee, for a maximum credit of $2,444 per employee for the first year of employment. Employers' deductions for wages must be reduced by the amount of the credit.

Individuals must be employed for at least 90 days or have completed at least 120 hours.

How to Apply for TJTC. To apply for the credit, the individual with a disability contacts the local state-federal vocational rehabilitation office to receive a voucher. The employer completes a portion of the voucher and mails it to the nearest local employment service office. That agency will send the employer a certificate that validates the tax credit. The employer uses this certificate when filing federal tax forms.

For more information on TJTC, contact the local state-federal vocational rehabilitation agency or the local employment service office.

Vocational Rehabilitation Programs

The federal-state vocational rehabilitation program has a 71-year history of helping people with disabilities enter the competitive work force. Vocational rehabilitation agencies can be found in most cities. They are a resource for employers seeking to recruit qualified people with disabilities. They may also be helpful regarding job accommodations. They can conduct job analysis and provide rehabilitation engineering services for architectural barrier removal and work-site modifications.

An on-the-job training program can be set up with an employer for an individual client of vocational rehabilitation. The agency can help to pay the employee's wages for a limited time on a negotiated schedule. The position must be permanent, full time, and pay above minimum wage.

Job Training Partnership Act

The Job Training Partnership Act (JTPA) replaces the Comprehensive Employment and Training Act (CETA). The program is administered by the governor's office in each state. JTPA is a joint public-private sector venture to train and place individuals who are "economically disadvantaged" in the labor market. Disabled individuals can be considered economically disadvantaged if they meet the criteria set by the federal, state, or local welfare system.

JTPA can set up on-the-job training at a work site and reimburse an employer 50 percent of the first six months of wages for each eligible employee. Other JTPA services include: job recruiting, counseling in basic work skills, customized training programs, and services to those placed in unsubsidized jobs.

For more information, contact your local private industry council or chamber of commerce.

SITUATION ANALYSIS

Situation

Diana B. suffers from asthma, which she developed while working for her current employer. It can't always be controlled with medication, so it disrupts her job as a contract administrator. Now she must excuse herself from major negotiations and is embarrassed.

The problem can be corrected by purifying the air in Diana's office with a forced-air unit. However, it requires an outside purifier, which would add to the monthly electrical costs. The employer refuses on the basis of undue hardship.

Can Diana legally insist on a separate air purifier under the ADA? Can the employer deduct the expense of purchasing, installing, and maintaining the purifier from her salary?

Analysis. The ADA can probably help Diana. If she establishes her entitlement properly, she should be able to negotiate her biggest deal.

She must first show that she's covered by the ADA. It defines a disabled person as someone who:

1. Has a physical or mental impairment that substantially limits one or more major life activities.
2. Has a record of such impairment.
3. Is regarded as having the impairment.

Working is considered a "major life activity," and repeatedly interrupting major business negotiations qualifies as a "substantial limitation" on the work.

The employer must provide any reasonable accommodation, as long as it doesn't impose an undue hardship on the business or threaten the health or safety of other employees. In this example, the cost of installing a purifier is a modest $1,500; and the noise wouldn't bother other employees, so Diana's request would probably be considered reasonable.

The fact that the illness developed while Diana was working for this employer makes no difference. The ADA doesn't differentiate between preexisting conditions and those arising on the job—even if caused by it.

CHAPTER THIRTEEN

Accommodating
Specific Disabilities

Let's look at how some employers have dealt with major limiting conditions that cut across a variety of functions—lifting and carrying, sitting, manual tasks, mobility, hearing, seeing—as well as employment of workers with developmental disabilities. The information in this chapter is adapted from *Employers Are Asking About Accommodating Workers with Disabilities*, published by the President's Committee on Employment of People with Disabilities.

LIFTING AND CARRYING

No job is completely free from lifting or carrying tasks, yet these tasks can cause problems for people with heart conditions, spinal cord injuries, cerebral palsy, or limited stamina. One of the most common reasons for difficulty in lifting or carrying is injury to the lower back, which affects some 80 percent of the American population. It has been estimated that low back pain costs between $20 million and $30 million in worker's compensation costs and lost productivity.

The following guidelines for job modifications can help to prevent back injuries and minimize their limitations.

Problems and Solutions

1. Objects are too large or heavy.
    *   Assign the task to more than one worker.
    *   Distribute the load into more than one container.

- Use assistive equipment such as carts or overhead cranes.
- Modify the tasks.
- Provide handles or hooks to assure a firm grip on objects.
- Provide smooth flat surfaces to allow for sliding rather than lifting.
- Use lightweight containers; change container shape.
- Use large-wheeled carts to minimize effort.

2. Objects are not accessible.
   - Where possible, locate objects from 20 to 52 inches above floor.
   - Provide height-adjustable work surfaces, storage, and seating.
   - For object assembly, ensure access to all sides of worktable; use turntables if necessary.
   - Locate objects at about the same level to which they must be lifted.
   - Minimize reaching into deep storage containers through use of spring-loaded or sloped bottoms.

3. Frequency or duration of lifting/carrying causes fatigue.
   - Allow more time to complete task.
   - Reduce frequency of task.
   - Rotate workers to limit exposure to stress.
   - Provide rest periods.
   - Control temperature extremes.

Scenario

In a television repair shop, a worker with limited strength in his legs had to regularly lift television sets from the floor to his worktable and then back down onto the floor for removal. Because each technician at this shop works independently, asking a coworker to help would disrupt overall productivity. As an alternative, the company purchased a freestanding electronic platform lift that would raise and lower the sets for him. The device cost approximately $450.

SITTING

Seating accommodations should take into account the nature of the disability (e.g., paralysis, arthritis, hip injury) as well as the job itself. Because seating determines posture and movement patterns, a well-designed chair can even prevent disabilities. Studies indicate that a good chair can add up to 40 minutes of production to a workday. The mechanics of sitting include awareness of balance, hip and leg pressure, and alignment of the vertebral column. The preferred solution among ergonomics professionals is a fully adjustable chair.

The following job design guidelines can help to prevent physical problems and maximize productivity in the workplace.

Problem and Solutions

An employee complains of excessive fatigue at the end of the workday.

- Seating should allow the user's feet to either touch the floor or a footrest on the chair. The seat should be height adjustable to between 14 and 20 inches above the floor.
- The backrest on the chair should be adjustable for both angle and height to provide appropriate lumbar support.

Scenario

A copy machine operator with arthritis was having difficulty reaching up and across the machine to perform certain tasks. Because the machine was too complex to alter, the operator's working height was changed with a height-adjustable stool. The stool provided full back support and a platform for her feet. It cost about $350.

MANUAL TASKS

Poorly designed work patterns, vibration, and repetitive hand motions can contribute to chronic hand, arm, shoulder, and back problems. Job task analyses, time-and-motion studies, and equipment inspections can help an employer determine what accommodations will be most productive for workers who have trouble performing manual tasks.

The following modification guidelines illustrate different ways in which an employer can enable people with manual limitations to continue on the job.

Problems and Solutions

1. Task simplification.
    - Store tools and equipment for a particular task in one place.
    - Change task sequences to increase efficiency.
    - Provide assistive devices where needed.
    - Eliminate nonessential movements; combine essential movements.
2. Minimize the need for hand and forearm strength.
    - Suspend or counterbalance heavy tools.
    - Provide tools that can be used in either hand.
    - For single-hand tools, grip span should be between 2 and 4 inches.
    - Design hand tools for operation with a straight wrist. The rule is "bend the tool, not the wrist."
3. For severely disabled workers, use electronic equipment to simulate manual tasks.
    - Provide electronic equipment with voice or touch control devices.
    - Install electric tools.

Scenario

A manufacturing assembler complained of chronic carpal tunnel syndrome in his wrists and hands. A thorough job analysis revealed that repeated reaching for parts in boxes created constant wrist-bending demands on the worker. The workstation was redesigned with shallow bins so that parts could be stored on each side of the worker and at table height. The individual was encouraged to take breaks at regular intervals. A $100 job accommodation for the new bins improved the worker's productivity and decreased sick leave.

MOBILITY

Mobility in the workplace must take into account all areas related to work, including the parking lot, restrooms, cafeteria, and workstations. It is a good idea to involve employees in planning mobility accommodations.

Following are some general guidelines for accommodating people with mobility impairments.

Problems and Solutions

1. Common areas and pathways to work.
    *   Parking spaces near the building should be reserved for people with disabilities; spaces should be at least 13 feet wide to allow for wheelchairs or van lifts.
    *   Entrance doors should have a clear opening of 32 inches (36 inches in some states); use accessible door hardware.
    *   Ramps or lifts may be needed over changes in floor level.
    *   All storage and shelving should be accessible from a seated position. Provide storage for crutches, walkers, and canes.

Scenario

On evaluating the work site of a secretary in a wheelchair, it was observed that the calculator was located on a coworker's desk and the computer terminal was at yet another workstation. Maneuvering the wheelchair between the desks was difficult, so the employer organized the equipment on a turntable at the secretary's workstation. This made her more efficient, and it removed the safety hazard from cords draped across the floor. The turntable cost about $400.

HEARING

There are 15 to 20 million hearing-impaired people in the United States. Between 350,000 and 2 million of them have total hearing loss. Major modifications to the work area are not usually necessary to accommodate hearing-impaired workers or job applicants. For the most part, communicating with them is a matter of sensitivity and common sense.

Accommodation Ideas

• Train immediate coworkers in American Sign Language. The basics can be learned in a few hours, so the expense is minimal. Some local organizations provide sign language classes.

• Designate another employee or ask for volunteers to keep the person aware of informal communications such as the office "grapevine" and to alert him or her in an emergency.

• Use signaling devices such as a flashing light for customer service or a telephone flasher that signals when the phone rings.

• Provide vibrating pagers.

• Minimize vibrations in the work area. They distort sounds received by a hearing aid.

• Use sound amplification devices (volume control, high-intensity ring) on telephones.

• More than 100,000 telecommunication devices for the deaf (TDDs) are in use today. In the past, these devices could be used only if the person on the other end of the phone call also had a TDD to receive the printed message. The Americans with Disabilities Act eliminates this restriction by requiring telephone companies to provide relay services whereby a deaf person can use a TDD or type a message that is converted by the phone company into an audible form. Similarly, voice communications to a hearing-impaired recipient are relayed from voice to TDD. TDDs cost from $150 to about $1,000.

Scenario

A federal agency accommodated a hearing-impaired distribution clerk who was asked the same routine questions by other employees by providing six question signs that the hearing employees could use to indicate their questions and 12 preprinted cards that the employee could use in answering.

SEEING

Some 14 million Americans are visually impaired, defined as unable to read regular-size print, even with glasses. About 800,000 people are legally blind, which means that even with glasses they can see something no better at 20 feet than someone with normal sight can see at 200 feet. It is estimated that more than 80 percent of the 32,000 jobs listed in the *Dictionary of*

Occupational Titles can be performed by visually-impaired workers with proper job analysis, training, and equipment. Nevertheless, studies show that 70 percent of the working-age people with serious vision problems are unemployed or underemployed.

People who have trouble seeing need environmental cues to help them navigate around the workplace. Lights, strong colors, or red markers can help locate machine controls, mechanical tools, stair treads, light switches, and doorknobs. Consistent location of furniture and equipment can map the path of travel.

Following are examples of the many tools and devices on the market that make it possible for people with visual impairments to accomplish almost any task.

Electronic Aids (Approximate Prices)

- Safety saw guide for blind carpenters (under $25).
- Talking calculator (under $40).
- Telephone that stores up to 200 names and phone numbers and automatically dials a number upon a spoken command (under $200).
- Braille printer for computer ($1,000).
- Computer voice commands that work with most word-processing programs ($250).
- Talking lap computer with braille command system (under $3,000).
- Braille pocket folding tape measure ($13).
- Various "talking" measuring tools ($150 to $500).
- Illuminated magnifiers ($20 to $50).
- Portable print enlarger ($950 to $1,800).
- Enlarged numbers that fit over a touchtone phone (under $15).
- Combination lamp and magnifying glass ($35).
- Voice-recognition system that allows one to convert spoken commands into 64 different computer commands ($150).

Administrative Accommodations

- ***Physical orientation.*** A blind or visually-impaired person might need help in becoming oriented to the workplace. The new employee should be taken around the facility to locate entrances, exits, and restrooms. The location of tools and office supplies should be pointed out and the employee should be encouraged to touch objects.
- ***Employee education.*** Supervisors and coworkers should be informed of the new employee's needs and qualifications before the person begins work. It will be much easier to enlist their cooperation if they understand the situation in advance. However, if the vision problem is not obvious,

coworkers should not be informed until after the person has voluntarily disclosed the problem.

Scenario

A blind machinist's job involved machining parts for hydraulic cylinders. For under $300, the company provided her with a braille micrometer to measure the diameter of precision metal shafts.

A DuPont employee who lost his sight from an optic nerve tumor was able to return to his job as a computer programmer thanks to a voice synthesizer that allowed his computer to talk. The cost was under $1,000.

MENTAL RETARDATION

Some 6 million Americans are mentally retarded. More than 90 percent of them are only mildly retarded (an IQ of between 51 and 70) and can perform all types of work without anyone recognizing their retardation.

Some people feel that retarded workers should not be mixed with other workers, but experience has proven that they generally can work side by side with nondisabled employees without difficulty. With adequate training, a worker who has a developmental disability should not require any extra supervision. As with all employees, supervisors must be sensitive and straightforward in dealing with them.

Scenario

• As reported in *The New York Times*, the owner of a commercial laundry in Russellville, Arkansas, found it hard to find people who would start at the minimum wage. He began recruiting workers from the Russell Skills Center, a local sheltered workshop for people with retardation and mental disabilities, to do folding, sorting, and processing of laundry. Today, 5 of the company's 16 employees come from the center. The agency provides coaches for the workers until they learn their routines.

• To keep up production, Kreonite, a Wichita-based manufacturer of darkroom equipment, recently brought in a team of mentally disabled workers from a local sheltered workshop, the Kansas Elks Training Center for the Handicapped. With about 15 percent of its 240-member work force consisting of people with disabilities, Kreonite employs a full-disability coordinator to supervise these workers. The company's senior vice-president maintains that workers, disabled or not, need supervisors. Kreonite just employs one who is skilled in dealing with disabilities.

CHAPTER FOURTEEN

Enforcement of
ADA Employment Regulations

REMEDIES

The remedies and procedures provided by Title I of the Americans with Disabilities Act (ADA) are the same as those available under Title VII of the Civil Rights Act of 1964 to people discriminated against on the basis of their race, religion, sex, or national origin. These remedies include:

- Hiring or reinstatement
- Promotion
- Increase in wages or benefits
- Back pay, front pay, and other wage adjustments
- Adjustments in policies and procedures
- Monetary awards and fines, including payment of attorney's fees, expert witness fees, and court costs
- Increased reporting requirements
- Oversight and monitoring of employment practices
- Prevention of retaliation
- Other administrative and civil remedies

Damage awards are capped at $50,000 against firms with 15 to 100 employees and at $300,000 for larger firms. The caps are the same as those in Title VII of the Civil Rights Act, and Congress is considering removing them.

A violation of Title VII can be established in one of two ways: by proving intentional discrimination or by proving that a particular employer policy has a disparate impact on a defined group. A plaintiff cannot build a disparate impact case based on *general* employment practices.

Because the ADA adopts all of Title VII's remedial provisions, any amendments to Title VII are fully applicable to the ADA. For instance, the ADA itself says nothing about the right to a jury trial, but the Civil Rights Reform Act of 1990 amended Title VII and allowed jury trials in cases alleging intentional discrimination and seeking compensatory or punitive damages. This provision will apply to the ADA as well.

A plaintiff who lodges a disability-related discrimination charge cannot bypass the administrative remedies of Title VII and go directly to court under Title I of the ADA. He or she must follow the same procedures and secure the same remedies as women and minorities do under Title VII. Nevertheless, the ADA does not limit the person's access to the rights, remedies, and procedures of other federal and state laws.

The ADA encourages the informal resolution of claims through settlement negotiations, conciliation, facilitation, mediation, fact-finding, minitrials, and arbitration. However, the use of alternative methods is voluntary. A person doesn't have to exhaust the informal procedures in order to pursue the remedies provided for in the ADA.

ENFORCEMENT: ROLE OF EEOC AND STATE AGENCIES

Responsibility for enforcing Title I of the ADA rests with the federal Equal Employment Opportunity Commission (EEOC), the administrative agency that enforces almost all major federal employment legislation.

In addition to the federal laws, 42 of the 50 states have enacted their own fair employment laws and have created state equal employment opportunity (EEO) agencies to enforce them. When a complaint is filed with the EEOC, that agency will defer the complaint to the state agency, if one exists. Practically speaking, most employment discrimination complaints are investigated and resolved not by the EEOC but by the state agencies. Most state EEO agencies have ongoing contracts with the EEOC under which they are paid for each EEOC-deferred complaint they handle.

The federal EEOC usually adopts the determination of the state EEO agency as its own decision. Only in rare cases will the EEOC agree to look at a complaint that was dismissed by the state agency for lack of probable cause.

For Title VII actions under federal law, charges must be filed with the EEOC within 180 days of the alleged discriminatory act. In deferral states with approved enforcement agencies, statutes of limitation range from a minimum of 30 days to a maximum period of one year (see Table 14.1). An untimely charge will be dismissed no matter how strong the case is.

Table 14.1   State EEO Agencies and Statutes of Limitations Under State EEO Laws

State and State EEO Law	*State EEO Law Y/N*	*Provides for Investigation and Public Hearing Procedure—Y/N*	*Statute of Limitations Under State EEO Laws*
Alabama	N	. . .	. . .
Alaska Alaska State Laws Against Discrimination	Y	Y	300 days
Arizona Arizona Civil Rights Act	Y	Y	180 days
Arkansas	N	. . .	. . .
California California Fair Employment Practices and Housing Act	Y	Y	1 year
Colorado Colorado Antidiscrimination Act	Y	Y	6 months
Connecticut Connecticut Fair Employment Practices Act	Y	Y	180 days
Delaware Delaware Fair Employment Practices Act	Y	Y	90 days
Florida Florida Human Rights Act	Y	Y	180 days
Georgia No comprehensive statute	Y	Y	180 days
Hawaii Hawaii Fair Employment Practices Act	Y	Y	30 days
Idaho Idaho Fair Employment Practices Act	Y	N	1 year

Table 14.1   (Continued)

State and State EEO Law	State EEO Law Y/N	Provides for Investigation and Public Hearing Procedure—Y/N	Statute of Limitations Under State EEO Laws
Illinois			
Illinois Human Rights Act	Y	Y	180 days
Indiana			
Indiana Civil Rights Law	Y	Y	90 days
Iowa			
Iowa Civil Rights Law	Y	Y	180 days
Kansas			
Kansas Act Against Discrimination	Y	Y	6 months
Kentucky			
Kentucky Fair Employment Practices Act	Y	Y	180 days
Louisiana	N	. . .	. . .
Maine			
Maine Human Rights Act	Y	N	6 months
Maryland			
Maryland Fair Employment Practices Act	Y	Y	6 months
Massachusetts			
Massachusetts Fair Employment Practices Law	Y	Y	6 months
Michigan			
Michigan Civil Rights Act	Y	Y	180 days
Minnesota			
Minnesota Human Rights Act	Y	Y	300 days
Mississippi	N	. . .	. . .
Missouri			
Missouri Fair Employment Practices Act	Y	Y	180 days
Montana			
Montana Human Rights Act	Y	Y	180 days

Table 14.1 (*Continued*)

State and State EEO Law	State EEO Law Y/N	Provides for Investigation and Public Hearing Procedure—Y/N	Statute of Limitations Under State EEO Laws
Nebraska			
Nebraska Fair Employment Practices Act	Y	Y	180 days
Nevada			
Nevada Fair Employment Practices Act	Y	Y	180 days
New Hampshire			
New Hampshire Law Against Discrimination	Y	Y	180 days
New Jersey			
New Jersey Law Against Discrimination	Y	Y	180 days
New Mexico			
New Mexico Human Rights Act	Y	Y	1 year
New York			
New York Human Rights Law	Y	Y	1 year
North Carolina	N	. . .	. . .
North Dakota	N	. . .	. . .
Ohio			
Ohio Fair Employment Practices Law	Y	Y	6 months
Oklahoma			
Oklahoma Civil Rights Act	Y	Y	180 days
Oregon			
Oregon Fair Employment Practices Act	Y	Y	1 year
Pennsylvania			
Pennsylvania Human Relations Act	Y	Y	90 days
Rhode Island			
Rhode Island Fair Employment Practices Act	Y	Y	1 year

Table 14.1   (Continued)

State and State EEO Law	State EEO Law Y/N	Provides for Investigation and Public Hearing Procedure—Y/N	Statute of Limitations Under State EEO Laws
South Carolina			
South Carolina Human Affairs Law	Y	Y	180 days
South Dakota			
South Dakota Human Relations Act	Y	Y	180 days
Tennessee			
Tennessee Fair Employment Practices Law	Y	Y	180 days
Texas			
Texas Commission on Human Rights Act	Y	N	180 days
Utah			
Utah Antidiscriminatory Act	Y	Y	180 days
Vermont	N	. . .	. . .
Virginia	N	. . .	. . .
Washington			
Washington Law Against Discrimination	Y	Y	6 months
West Virginia			
West Virginia Human Rights Act	Y	Y	90 days
Wisconsin			
Wisconsin Fair Employment Act	Y	Y	300 days
Wyoming			
Wyoming Fair Employment Practices Act	Y	Y	90 days
District of Columbia			
District of Columbia Human Rights Law	Y	Y	1 year

Source: Reprinted with permission from *The Employee Termination Handbook*, edited by J. G. Allen. New York: John Wiley & Sons, 1986, pp. 172–174.

Procedurally, Title VII of the 1964 Civil Rights Act is one of the more complicated statutes on the books. Under most federal laws, a plaintiff may go directly into federal court. But a Title VII plaintiff must first file a complaint with his or her state EEO agency, if one exists. That agency then has exclusive jurisdiction over the complaint for 60 days.

In deferral states, charges must be filed under *both* federal and state law. Even though most federal EEOC complaints are deferred to state EEO agencies, that does not mean the complaint has been filed under state law.

If a person mistakenly assumes that he or she has also filed under state law, the statute of limitations under the state law may expire. In fact, it sometimes happens that the statute of limitations expires on a state cause of action at the same time that the state EEO agency is in the process of investigating a deferred federal complaint.

PROCEDURES FOR LODGING AN ADA COMPLAINT

What actually happens when someone files a complaint alleging discrimination on the basis of a disability? Let's follow the process step by step.

Private Settlement

In the face of an enormous caseload, EEO agencies encourage early settlement between employer and employee. From the employer's point of view, an early settlement is generally less expensive than a later one, and it is certainly less expensive than losing an EEO lawsuit. If an employer agrees to settle before the agency begins its investigation, the complaint will be dismissed as having "no probable cause." A settlement that's negotiated *after* the investigation is completed is framed as a "conciliation agreement" (discussed below). This document records the fact that the investigation *did* disclose probable cause to support an allegation of unlawful discrimination. The EEOC maintains a file of all prior findings of probable cause.

Settlement prior to the investigation is achieved by direct communication between the parties. The agency need not be involved in this process. The settlement is put in writing, and the employee is obligated to withdraw the complaint.

Investigative Process

When a complaint is filed with the state EEO agency, the agency sends a copy to the employer along with an investigatory questionnaire that has to be completed within a specified amount of time. If the dispute cannot be resolved, the agency will either file suit against the employer or issue a "right to sue" letter that allows the plaintiff to bring a Title VII action in federal court within 90 days.

It is important to remember that even though the EEOC is a federal agency, filing a complaint with the EEOC is not the same as bringing it in federal court. The complaint to the agency is not automatically transformed into a federal court complaint.

Fact-Finding Conference

If the agency decides to proceed with the investigation, the next step is a fact-finding conference before an agency investigator. Most investigators are working under heavy caseloads, so a hiatus of several months between the receipt of the employer's response to the questionnaire and the scheduling of the conference is common.

The conference is the first opportunity for the employee and the employer to confront each other in the presence of an investigator. The employer's attorney may attend the conference but is not allowed to cross-examine the complainant or witnesses. Counsel's role is to direct the scope of the questions asked by the investigator and to present the employer's defense.

Requests for Information

An employer must provide any information that is required by state and federal regulations. Refusal to do so will almost guarantee a finding of probable cause. Performance appraisals are usually relevant to these proceedings, but employers sometimes keep only the most recent ones. Make sure you have *all* of them in your files. There is nothing more defeating to an employer's defense of a claim than 10 years' worth of "excellent" performance appraisals.

Conciliation Process

When the investigation is complete, the investigating commissioner will decide whether there is probable cause to believe that the employer has discriminated unlawfully against the employee. If there is no probable cause, the complaint will be dismissed.

If probable cause is found, the EEO agency will try to resolve the matter through a formal process called "conciliation." The conciliation agreement states the terms of the settlement and affirms that the complainant had probable cause for taking action.

Administrative Hearing

If conciliation fails, the matter will be decided at an administrative hearing before an administrative law judge of the state EEO agency. Although less formal than a court proceeding, the administrative hearing is similar to a trial in that there is examination and cross-examination of witnesses and introduction of documentary evidence such as personnel files.

Unlike a judge, an administrative judge has no enforcement powers of his or her own. However, an administrative judge has greater power to participate in the hearing than a judge has to participate in a court trial. The administrative judge is not restricted to simply making decisions on procedural questions but may actively engage in examination of witnesses.

The administrative hearing is not held in a court but usually in one of the offices of the state EEO agency. Prior to the hearing, the administrative law judge knows nothing of the case except for the initial complaint and the answer. The hearing itself is conducted without any reference to the investigation. Although an attorney is not required, most employers bring one along.

When the hearing is concluded, the administrative law judge will send a recommended decision to the parties or their attorneys, with notification that they can submit written objections to the decision within a specified period of time. The issuance of a recommended decision is generally the last involvement of the administrative law judge in the matter.

The findings of the administrative law judge are subject to the ultimate decision of the commissioner or the administrative chief of that agency. If the complaint is sustained, as it usually is, the agency will order legal relief to the employee, including back pay and reinstatement.

RELATIONSHIP OF ADA TO OTHER LAWS

State Laws

State laws can substantially increase the damages a private plaintiff collects in an ADA lawsuit. The ADA does not preempt any state law or municipal ordinance that provides greater protection for individuals with disabilities than those afforded by the ADA. Many state handicapped laws allow for added damages, although the exact types of damages provided vary from state to state. For example, the New Jersey Law Against Discrimination allows for pain and suffering, emotional distress, and punitive damages in addition to the federal remedies. Oregon law provides compensation for emotional distress or "impaired personal dignity," while Tennessee's law provides for damages for "humiliation and embarrassment." Lawsuits that combine actions based on the ADA and state handicapped laws are allowed only under certain circumstances.[1]

---

[1] James Frierson, *Employer's Guide to the Americans with Disabilities Act* (Washington, DC: Bureau of National Affairs, 1992), 209–210.

Rehabilitation Act of 1973

Those employed by or seeking employment with the federal government are protected under Section 501 of the Rehabilitation Act of 1973.

Sections 503 and 504 of the Rehabilitation Act regulate private employers and state/local government agencies that receive federal contracts or federal grants in excess of $2,500. The U.S. Department of Labor's Office of Federal Contract Compliance Programs is responsible for enforcing federal contract provisions.

Following are examples of how each law would apply in different situations in which the employer is a federal contractor or receives federal financial assistance:

- If the employer holds a federal contract for $5,000 but has only 10 employees, you are protected under Section 503 of the Rehabilitation Act.
- If the employer receives a federal research grant for $10,000 and has 20 employees, you are protected under Section 504 of the Rehabilitation Act.
- If the employer has a federal contract for $1,000 and has 50 employees, you are protected under Title I of the ADA.

Because the EEOC is responsible for enforcing both the ADA and the Rehabilitation Act of 1973, the law stipulates that administrative complaints filed under either piece of legislation must be dealt with in a way that avoids duplication of efforts or conflicting standards. Agencies with enforcement authority are expected to coordinate their efforts.

A TIDE OF LITIGATION?

On March 15, 1993, a federal jury created a legal milestone when it awarded $572,000 to Charles Wessel, a 59-year-old Oak Lawn, Illinois, man who was fired from a security company because he had terminal brain cancer. The verdict is the first in the nation to result from a lawsuit brought against a private employer by the EEOC under the Americans with Disabilities Act. The company was ordered to pay $500,000 in punitive damages, $50,000 in compensatory damages, and $22,000 in back pay. Wessel can keep only $222,000 of the total award because of a $200,000 cap on damages.

This is the first of some 15,000 job bias complaints the EEOC expects to receive in the ADA's first year alone. But because of budget constraints, the commission may not be able to hire the 250 new compliance officers it expects to need to investigate complaints under the ADA, so enforcement is likely to be slow.

Litigation is a powerful tool, but let's hope it's a last resort. Paul

Marchand, chairman of the Consortium for Citizens with Disabilities, a lobbying group in Washington, sums it up this way: "We are not out to clobber anybody. We hope it [litigation] would be the last resort. It makes no sense to put businesses out of business."[2]

TYPICAL CHARGES AND DEFENSES

The recap below is adapted from a manual published by the Bureau of National Affairs.[3]

CHARGE: A less-qualified person is hired over a more-qualified disabled person.

DEFENSE: After considering all reasonable accommodations, the employer must prove that the disabled person is less qualified.

CHARGE: Discrimination in employer-provided health or life insurance.

DEFENSE: The employer must prove that the limitation or denial of coverage is based upon normal insurance industry standards of risk, including exclusion for preexisting conditions. It is not necessary to show that all medical conditions are covered equally as long as the benefits are the same for all employees in the complainant's job category.

CHARGE: A job applicant or employee is discriminated against because of past drug use.

DEFENSE: The employer has two possible lines of defense here: (1) to show that the individual is still using drugs or (2) to show that treatment was based upon valid job criteria such as work quality, productivity standards, or attendance requirements.

CHARGE: A company uses job qualifications or employment tests to screen out qualified disabled people.

DEFENSE: The company must prove that its standards and tests measure essential job skills that are consistent with business necessity, and that reasonable accommodations were provided to allow the applicant to show his or her qualifications.

CHARGE: An applicant is unable to interview effectively for a job or take a qualifying examination either because of physical barriers or the format of the test.

DEFENSE: Defenses in this realm are limited because all employment tests and selection criteria must be administered in a way that does not automat-

---

[2]Peter Kilborn, "Change Likely as Law on Bias to Disabled Takes Effect." *New York Times,* 19 July 1992, sec. 1.

[3]Frierson, *Employer's Guide to the Americans with Disabilities Act,* 201–206.

ically screen out disabled people. The employer can either show that the person never attempted to qualify for the job or that the applicant did not ask for any accommodations.

CHARGE: An employer asks about health, disability, or past medical problems before making a job offer.

DEFENSE: The employer must prove that the questions related only to the applicant's ability to perform *essential job functions.* Employers are permitted to test for illegal drug use before making a job offer because current drug users are not a protected class under the ADA's definition of disability.

CHARGE: An employer requires a physical examination after making a tentative offer of employment and uses the information to screen out an applicant with a disability.

DEFENSE: The employer must prove that: (1) the examination was required of all employees, (2) any resulting decision was based upon legitimate proof that the person could not effectively and safely perform the essential tasks of the job, and (3) the information was kept confidential.

CHARGE: A person with AIDS is denied employment.

DEFENSE: The employer must either prove that the decision was not based upon the medical condition or that the condition created a health or safety risk to coworkers or customers. The latter is very difficult to prove, even in the case of food service workers or elementary school teachers. It might be a viable defense in some health care jobs.

CHARGE: A worker is denied a promotion because of his inability to perform certain job tasks.

DEFENSE: The employer must prove that the tasks in question are essential duties of the job and that eliminating them would change the fundamental nature of the job, lower productivity, or produce a poorer result.

CHARGE: An employer refuses to provide a reasonable accommodation for a disabled employee.

DEFENSE: The employer must show that the accommodation would create an undue hardship on the business, would present a threat to health or safety, or would not enable the person to perform the essential duties of the job.

CHARGE: A company segregates workers with disabilities and classifies them in a way that lowers their status in the company.

DEFENSE: Usually none. Different rates of pay, separate seniority lists, or separate physical facilities based upon disability are illegal. However, an employer may limit a disabled person to one section of the facility if the structural changes needed to improve access to other sections would present an undue hardship.

CHARGE: Employer does not provide information on the ADA.

DEFENSE: An employer must display the current "Consolidated EEO Poster," which includes information on the ADA, in a place where job applicants and employees would be expected to see it. The posters are available in large print and braille.

CHARGE: A business's goods and services are not physically accessible to customers or clients.

DEFENSE: If the building was constructed before January 26, 1993, or renovated before January 26, 1992, the business must show that the necessary changes were not readily achievable. If the building was constructed for first occupancy after January 6, 1993, or major modifications were begun after January 26, 1992, the structure must comply with the regulations promulgated by the U.S. attorney general.

CHARGE: Work areas, cafeterias, restrooms, water fountains, and other common areas in the workplace are not physically accessible to workers with disabilities.

DEFENSE: If the building was not completed after January 26, 1993, or substantially renovated since January 26, 1992, the company must prove that the cost of making changes would present an *undue burden*. If the structure was built or renovated after these dates, the only defense would be compliance with the U.S. attorney general's accessibility regulations.

SITUATION ANALYSES

Situation No. 1

Kate O. has an acute parathesia that immobilizes her left arm several times a year. As a draftsperson, this interferes with her productivity. However, she has learned to use a number of mechanical devices to get the work done.

She doesn't mention her disability to her prospective employer. She gets hired and then buys the equipment she will need when the paralysis occurs.

A few weeks into the job her arm starts bothering her, but she is afraid to bring her adaptive equipment into the office. Her supervisor is very overbearing and is likely to fire her for not disclosing the problem when she was hired. He has asked her to document her need for the mechanical devices.

Was Kate required to disclose her disability upon being hired to enforce her right to the job now? Can she enforce a right to have the employer pay for the equipment? Must she document the need? Can she take time off with pay to file and pursue a charge of discrimination?

Analysis. Kate was under no duty to disclose the paralysis upon being hired, so her rights under the ADA are not affected.

If the mechanical devices are reasonable in cost, they would be considered a "reasonable accommodation" and the employer would be required to pay for them. What's reasonable? That depends on the circumstances. If Kate were a senior engineer, a higher cost might be considered reasonable by the EEOC. If she were a drafting trainee, a lower one might be considered reasonable.

She would have to document the need to her supervisor if requested—and certainly to the EEOC. She has no right to time off with pay to pursue a charge of discrimination.

Situation No. 2

James Q. is paralyzed in one leg and uses a walker.

While he is interviewing, he slips and falls. The interviewer asks him how he will maneuver in the job of a production expediter. James is embarrassed but insists that he can do the job. Then the interviewer tells him the company's worker's compensation insurance carrier is already threatening to cancel the policy. The rates have become so high that the company may have to move its production overseas.

James has a major worker's compensation case pending against his former employer. The state worker's comp statute makes employers liable for additional benefits if an employee is assigned to a job that jeopardizes health or safety.

Must James mention the claim? Can the employer refuse to hire him because of it? Must James be hired and given a different job?

Analysis. This is a difficult situation for both parties.

As a federal law, the ADA supersedes state worker's compensation laws. This locks the employer into hiring James. Further, he can file a charge under the ADA and a worker's compensation claim simultaneously if discrimination and injury occur after he is hired.

Under the ADA, James doesn't have to reveal anything about the worker's comp claim until an offer is extended. A postoffer inquiry could result in the offer being revoked, but at least he can establish that the comp claim was the reason. The EEOC will help him once a charge is filed.

There is no requirement for the employer to assign James to another job or to dramatically alter the expediter duties.

Situation No. 3

Lisa F. is a partially sighted switchboard operator. She is able to read company telephone directories and regular print items.

During her interview, she was asked to read a public phone book. She couldn't do it, but otherwise the interview went well. She was told that she would be notified of the outcome within two weeks.

Three weeks have elapsed and Lisa has heard nothing. She calls the company anonymously and asks the operator whether the switchboard job entails reading phone books. The operator says it doesn't.

Should Lisa call the interviewer and point this out? Should she wait to see whether an offer is extended? If she is rejected, does she have the right to know why? If it's because she can't read a phone book, can she force the company to hire her?

Analysis. Although it's a high-risk strategy, I'd advise Lisa to make the call. If she's good-natured about nailing the interviewer, she'll probably get the job. Interviewers are administrators and avoid conflict wherever possible.

I recommend making the call before an offer is extended because it looks like Lisa won't receive an offer. If she waits until she's turned down to challenge the decision, the interviewer will have time to find a legal justification for it.

There's no law that requires an employer to give an applicant a reason for rejection. But if the interviewer tells her (preferably *writes* her) that the decision is based on her inability to read the phone book, Lisa can enforce her right to the job.

CHAPTER FIFTEEN

Title III: How Can You Succeed If You Can't Get In?

In Chapter 12, we noted that the reasonable accommodation requirement for employers under Title I of the Americans with Disabilities Act (ADA) calls for workplace changes in two broad areas: (1) operational and equipment-related modifications, and (2) structural modifications geared to "making existing facilities readily accessible to employees with disabilities."

The first requirement was covered in Chapter 12; the second point, concerning structural modifications, cuts across both Title I of the ADA, regulating employers, and Title III, regulating businesses. In this chapter and the next, we will outline the general requirements of Title III as well as specific architectural specifications for accessibility.

OVERVIEW OF TITLE III

Title III of the ADA took effect on January 26, 1992. Its general intent is to enable individuals with disabilities to participate more fully in the mainstream of society, with greater access to entertainment events, educational institutions, and commercial establishments ranging from restaurants to laundromats.

Title III imposes both affirmative and negative requirements on businesses:

- Nondiscrimination in providing goods and services.
- Modification of policies and procedures that discriminate against people with disabilities.
- Provision of auxiliary aids and services where needed.
- Removal of structural barriers if this is readily achievable.

Together, the law and its implementing regulations create a web of obligations designed to eliminate exclusion, segregation, and denial of opportunity on the basis of disabilities.

Let's examine these points one by one.

Nondiscrimination in Providing Goods and Services

Although the ADA grants persons with disabilities the right to participate in the goods and services offered in the marketplace, it does not require that such individuals achieve an identical result as those in the general population. For example, although a person who uses a wheelchair could not be excluded from an exercise program, the instructor doesn't have to ensure that the individual can perform every exercise that the nondisabled participants can.

Outright exclusion is the most blatant form of discrimination in providing goods and services, but discrimination also extends to practices such as adopting criteria that impose an additional burden on people with disabilities. A theater or restaurant, for example, may not require people who use wheelchairs to be accompanied by an attendant.

The law also stipulates that the goods and services must be provided in the "most integrated setting appropriate to the needs of the individual." In practical terms, this means that seating in a restaurant cannot restrict people with disabilities to a certain section and that designated wheelchair positions cannot be located only in the back row of an auditorium. It is also discriminatory for a public accommodation to provide different or separate goods and services to people with disabilities. A gymnasium might offer special classes for children with limited mobility, but it cannot restrict them to those classes.

Modification of Policies and Procedures

This requirement is broader than the reasonable accommodation provision in Title I of the ADA and, in essence, requires that businesses remain flexible when applying their rules so as not to exclude the disabled. Modifications are required unless they would fundamentally alter the nature of the goods or services provided.

Examples

- A department store may need to modify its policy of permitting only one person in a dressing room if an individual with a disability needs assistance from a companion.
- A store with checkout aisles must ensure that enough accessible aisles are kept open. If only one checkout aisle is accessible and that aisle is generally used for express service, one way of providing equivalent service is to allow people with mobility impairments to check out all of their purchases at the express aisle.
- A check-cashing requirement that a person have a driver's license for identification violates the ADA because it screens out people with disabilities who cannot drive.
- A restaurant or hotel that does not allow dogs must modify that rule for a service dog.
- A business need *not* expand its normal inventory to cater to individuals with disabilities. For example, stores are not expected to stock braille books.

Auxiliary Aids and Services

Businesses must provide whatever devices or services are needed to ensure that individuals with disabilities can enjoy the goods and services of a business. One of the most common of these aids is a telecommunication device for the deaf (TDD). Other examples include:

- Readers
- Braille documents
- Interpreters
- Telephone handset amplifiers
- Telephones compatible with hearing aids
- Closed captions
- Decoders
- Taped texts
- Audio recordings
- Large-print materials

Which of these aids is necessary depends upon the nature of the business and the nature of the disability. As with Title I, a business is not required to provide its patrons with personal devices such as wheelchairs or hearing aids, nor is it required to provide personal service such as assistance in eating or using restrooms.

Removal of Architectural Barriers in Existing Facilities

The obligation to remove architectural barriers is limited by what is "readily achievable," a standard that we'll discuss later in this chapter (see Figure 15.1 for list of common barriers found in existing facilities). Justice Department regulations mention the following examples of barrier removals that may be required under Title III:

- Installing ramps and grab bars
- Lowering telephones
- Repositioning paper towel dispensers
- Adding raised letters and braille markings on elevator controls
- Adding flashing alarms
- Widening doors
- Making curb cuts in sidewalks and entrances
- Eliminating turnstiles or providing an alternative path
- Designating accessible parking spaces
- Removing high-pile, low-density carpeting
- Installing hand controls for driving vehicles
- Insulating lavatory pipes under sinks to prevent burns
- Removing barriers in transportation vehicles

Examples _____

A business may be required to rearrange furniture and equipment, a restaurant may need to rearrange its tables, and a department store may have to adjust the layout of display racks and shelves. A bus company may have to install accessible luggage racks and special seats for disabled passengers.

Use of Alternative Methods

If the removal of a barrier is not readily achievable, a business must make its goods and services available through alternative methods. This might include providing help in retrieving items from densely packed display racks, coming to the door of a store to receive or return dry cleaning, or rotating movies between a first-floor theater and a comparable one on an upper floor.

In some cases, perhaps for security reasons, an alternative method may not be readily achievable. The rule does not require a cashier to leave his or her post to retrieve items for people who need help if there are no other employees on duty.

Figure 15.1   Identifying Common Barriers

Parking. Space is too narrow to permit transfer to wheelchair or crutches. Space is not level. A curb or step separates space from paved walk. Reserved sign is not visible.

Approach. Street between parking space and building entrance has no traffic light or curb cut at crossing. A step separates sidewalk and entrance level. Ramp is too steep for wheelchair.

Entrance. Doors are too narrow to admit wheelchair. Revolving doors operate while nearby swing doors are locked. Distance between outer and inner doors is too short. Excessive pressure is needed to operate doors.

Stairs. Steps have open risers or projecting nosings that can trip people using crutches. Handrail is too high or too low, or is difficult to grasp because of its size or shape.

Elevators. Entrance is too narrow to admit wheelchair. Door level is out of alignment with building floor. Controls for upper floors are out of reach. Buttons are flush, precluding unaided use by persons who are visually impaired. The audible arrival signal doesn't tell people whether cab is on the way up or down. Cab size is too small for wheelchair.

Floors. Floors between different parts of the building are not level and are connected by steps only. Floors are surfaced in slippery material or carpeted with deep-pile carpeting.

Restrooms. Restrooms on another floor are not connected by elevator. Double doors at entrance are situated so that wheelchair user must have both doors open at same time to pass through. Space is inadequate for turning wheelchair.

Water closet. Toilet stall door is too narrow to admit wheelchair. Door swings into the toilet stall. Stall has no grab bars. Water closet seat is too low or too high for transfer from wheelchair.

Lavatory. Clearance below bowl is too small to permit wheelchair to slide under. Hot water line is uninsulated. Towel bar, soap, and paper towel dispensers and disposal are out of reach. Mirror is out of line of vision.

Water fountain. Spout and controls are out of reach. Fountain is placed in alcove too narrow for wheelchair.

Coin-operated telephones. Telephone is set in a too-narrow enclosed booth. Coin slot, dial, and handset are out of reach. No amplification is available for persons who are hard of hearing.

Controls. Windows, draperies, heat and light controls, and fire alarms are situated out of reach of people in wheelchairs.

Hazards. Doors leading to boiler rooms and other hazardous spaces are not

Figure 15.1 *(Continued)*

identifiable by touch. Floor access panels or holes are left unprotected. Paving has gratings that snag wheelchair wheels. Signs and fixtures are hung so low that they are a danger to persons with blindness.

Alarms. Fire alarms are audible only, without accompanying visual alarm for people with hearing impairments. Exit signs are not distinct enough to be distinguished by people with partial sight. Other typical barriers at the work site include storage cabinets and shelves too high or too low; door swings that obstruct free movement of wheelchair; workbench or counter too low to permit wheelchair to slide under; no level station for wheelchair in auditorium; no existing auditorium seats removed to accommodate wheelchairs; aisles too narrow for wheelchairs; lockers inaccessible; cafeteria serving counters out of reach to people in wheelchairs; not enough leg clearance under restaurant tables.

Source: Reprinted with permission from *Employees Are Asking about Making the Workplace Accessible to Workers with Disabilities*, Washington, DC: President's Committee on Employment of People with Disabilities, 1991.

Who Is Regulated under Title III?

Title III affects a broad spectrum of businesses, from bowling alleys to daycare centers. It applies to public accommodations and commercial facilities as well as to public transportation provided by private entities. It does not cover government-operated facilities, private clubs, religious organizations, or owner-occupied inns with fewer than five rooms.

Large companies have had to comply with the law since January 26, 1992. For businesses with 25 or fewer employees and gross receipts of less than $1 million, the effective date was July 26, 1992. New buildings and businesses with 10 or fewer employees and gross revenues of less than $500,000 have until January 26, 1993.

What Is a Place of Public Accommodation?

Nearly all businesses that provide goods and services to the public fall within the ADA's definition of public accommodation. Congress did not enact a small business exemption to the public access provisions, so they apply fully to virtually all privately run businesses open to the public— regardless of size. There are 12 categories of public accommodations:

1. Hotels and other lodging places
2. Restaurants, bars, and other places serving food or drink
3. Movie theaters, concert halls, and stadiums

4. Convention centers, lecture halls, and other meeting places
5. Bakery shops, grocery stores, clothing stores, hardware stores, videotape rental stores, and other sales or rental establishments
6. Laundromats, dry cleaners, banks, barber and beauty shops, shoe repair shops, funeral parlors, gas stations, hospitals, offices of an accountant or lawyer, doctors' offices, and other service establishments
7. Terminals used for public transportation
8. Museums, libraries, and galleries
9. Park, zoos, and other places of recreation
10. Schools and other places of education
11. Day-care centers, senior centers, shelters, and other social service facilities
12. Gymnasiums, health clubs, and other places of exercise

The Title III requirements apply only to those portions of a public accommodation that are open to the public. If a person operates a dry cleaning business with living quarters in the back, the part that's used as a residence is exempt from coverage.

What Is a Commercial Facility?

Commercial facilities are an even broader group, encompassing all nonresidential facilities affecting commerce. Factories, warehouses, and office buildings are within this definition.

Businesses with fewer than 15 employees are not regulated by Title I's workplace accessibility requirements, but there is no size limitation on the Title III requirements applicable to commercial facilities.

Who Is Responsible—Landlord or Tenant?

Both the landlord and the tenant (the one who owns or operates a place of public accommodation) have responsibilities to remove barriers to accessibility, but they are not clearly defined. The responsibilities are not necessarily equal, and they may be allocated to the parties according to the lease.

If modifications of a physical structure are necessary as a reasonable accommodation, the legal duty remains with the employer-tenant. If the rental agreement prohibits the tenant from making the modifications, the employer-tenant must make a good-faith effort to gain permission from the landlord. If the landlord approves of the alterations but they are not completed, the tenant is in violation.

Generally, the tenant is responsible only for alterations in the *leased premises,* while the landlord is responsible for making readily achievable alterations in common areas such as the parking lot or building entrance.

It remains the duty of the employer or business tenant to provide any required auxiliary devices that are not part of the leased structure.[1]

Special Accessibility Requirements for Entities Offering Tests and Courses

To ensure that key gateways to education and employment are open to people with disabilities, Title III of the ADA also requires any private entity that offers examinations or courses related to applications, licensing, certification, or credentialing to offer them in a place and manner accessible to persons with disabilities or to offer alternative accessible arrangements. That means a course might have to be offered on videocassette, or an examination might have to be given at an individual's home. The principles here are much the same as those governing preemployment screening discussed in Chapter 2. The examinations themselves must reflect the individual's aptitude or achievement level rather than his or her impairment. The examinations for individuals with disabilities must be offered as often as other examinations and at locations that are equally convenient.

A person who requests this type of accommodation must provide advance notice and appropriate documentation. (This might include a letter from a physician or evidence of a prior diagnosis or accommodation.) The applicant cannot be charged for any modifications or aids needed for the examination.

EMPLOYER DEFENSES

The "Readily Achievable" Standard

The "readily achievable" standard is not as rigorous as the standards for undue burden or undue hardship. Readily achievable means easily accomplishable and able to be carried out without much difficulty or expense. Relevant factors include:

- Nature and cost of removal.
- Financial resources of the facility, number of employees, effect on expenses and resources, and impact on operations.
- Financial resources of the overall company, its size, and the number of facilities it operates.
- The company's operations, the nature of the work force, geo-

---

[1] James Frierson, *Employer's Guide to the Americans with Disabilities Act* (Washington, DC: Bureau of National Affairs, 1992), 42.

graphic separateness, administrative or fiscal relationship of the facilities to the parent company.

Costs. In general, costs will be an effective guide to determining whether an alteration is readily achievable. No magic cutoff number will provide a definite yes or no answer as to when a removal is readily achievable, because the size of the business is a significant factor. A $1,000 removal may be readily achievable for a large company but not for one that is smaller or less profitable.

One unanswered question in the law is whether a given alteration must be evaluated in isolation or along with similar alterations. For example, at a single facility or location, the widening of a door that would cost $500 might seem to be readily achievable. But if there are 50 other doors that must be widened at a similar cost, the $25,000 total might far exceed the limited concept of readily achievable for that particular business, especially if the business is relatively small.

Examples

Retail stores may consider lowering their shelves to remove an architectural barrier to people in wheelchairs. However, it may not be readily achievable if it results in a significant loss of selling space. In this case, it might be more reasonable to try a different style of display rack or to have sales staff available to assist customers.

Automatic teller machines could be lowered to be accessible to people in wheelchairs; however, if this is not readily achievable, an inexpensive ramp could be built to achieve the same result.

A public accommodation may not place a surcharge on an individual with a disability to cover the costs of providing auxiliary aids and services, removing barriers, or modifying policies and procedures. Likewise, charges may not be assessed for home delivery provided as an alternative to barrier removal unless home delivery is provided to all customers for a fee.

Fundamental Nature of the Business

A business can justify a refusal to modify its policies and procedures if the modifications would fundamentally alter the nature of the goods and services.

Example

A rehabilitation clinic that focuses on alcohol addiction would not have to treat an individual suffering from a drug dependency.

Undue Burden

Undue burden is a key concept in deciding whether a business is required to provide an auxiliary aid or service. The factors used to determine undue burden are essentially the same as those for the readily achievable standard or the undue hardship standard discussed in connection with Title I.

Following are some other points to consider in assessing a company's ability to provide an auxiliary aid or service.

• *Solvency.* Companies on the verge of bankruptcy may be able to demonstrate undue burden more readily than healthy, profitable ones.

• *Past efforts and expenditures.* To the extent that a company has already expended large sums in providing auxiliary aids and services or in removing barriers to equal access, additional expenditures may be more of a burden.

• *Level of use.* A very large expenditure for an aid that is not likely to be used much may be considered an undue burden. However, if you can demonstrate that an aid is essential to enjoyment of the service and would be used with at least some frequency, it should be provided.

• *Costs and consequences to disabled people if auxiliary aid is not provided.* The more serious the costs and results of denying an aid, the more difficult it becomes to show an undue burden.

• *Administrative burden.* In all likelihood, only administrative burdens that seriously threaten to disrupt the flow of services will be given any consideration. Inconveniences such as having to rearrange schedules probably will not go far in demonstrating an undue burden.

• *Other industry efforts.* To the extent that other comparable businesses in similar industries have provided auxiliary aids and services, it will be more difficult to show undue burden.[2]

Public Safety

A business can justify allegedly discriminatory exclusion if it is necessary for safe operation of the business or if the individual's participation would pose a direct threat to the health or safety of others.

Example _____

A truck rental company might justify a requirement that all persons renting certain sized trucks have a commercial vehicle license on the grounds of public safety.

---

[2] Zachary Fasman, *What Business Must Know About the ADA: 1992 Compliance Guide* (Washington, DC: U.S. Chamber of Commerce, 1992), 58.

On the other hand, the direct threat justification must establish that the risk to the health or safety of others cannot be eliminated by modifying policies and procedures or by providing auxiliary aids or services. The ADA prohibits safety-based exclusion of a broad class of individuals with no specific inquiry as to the individual situation.

U.S. Department of Justice regulations specify that in determining whether an individual poses a direct threat, a business must conduct "an individualized assessment, based on a reasonable judgment that relies on current medical knowledge or on the best available objective evidence." Some safety concerns have no factual or medical foundation and are based upon the kinds of stereotypes the ADA seeks to eliminate.

Example _____

Fears about the risk of associating with an HIV-infected individual in a setting where there is no reasonable possibility of contracting the disease would not justify exclusion.

SUBSTANTIAL ALTERATIONS AND NEW CONSTRUCTION

For new construction and substantial alterations or renovations of existing buildings, the ADA requires that the needs of individuals with disabilities be considered. The new or renovated facility must be "readily accessible to and usable by individuals with disabilities, including individuals who use wheelchairs." This applies both to commercial facilities, which include places of employment, and to public accommodations.

This part of the ADA does not pertain to the construction or redesign of an individual workstation. That would fall under the Title I requirement for reasonable accommodation.

Also, in both new construction and alterations, businesses are not required to install elevators in facilities that are less than three stories or that have less than 3,000 square feet per floor.

Alterations

The ADA's requirements for alterations apply only to alterations that are otherwise planned. A business does not have to undertake wholesale renovation of its facilities beyond the removal of the architectural and communication barriers discussed in Chapter 12.

When alterations are made that affect areas of the facility containing a "primary function" of the business, the path of travel to the altered area and to restrooms, telephones, and drinking fountains in that area must also be readily accessible and usable unless the cost would be disproportionate to the overall alteration. According to Justice Department regulations, a cost is considered disproportionate if it exceeds 20 percent of the cost of the alteration to the primary function area.

Where cost is disproportionate, the alteration may be made in another way. And even if the cost of full compliance is disproportionate, partial compliance is expected. In this case, the first priority is an accessible entrance.

What Areas Contain a Primary Function? The law defines a primary function as "a major activity for which the facility is intended." The dining room of a cafeteria is an example of an area containing a primary function. A utility room in an office building probably would *not* be considered a primary function area. Justice Department regulations mention the following alterations as involving primary function areas:

- Remodeling merchandise display or employee work areas in a department store
- Replacing an inaccessible floor surface in the customer service or employee work area of a bank
- Redesigning the assembly line of a factory
- Installing a computer center in an accounting firm

Readily Accessible and Usable. This standard, which also applies to new construction, does not require that every part of a facility be accessible. It is generally applied to:

- Parking areas
- Routes to and from the facility
- Entrances
- Restrooms
- Water fountains
- Public use areas

A narrow exception to the accessibility requirement exists in situations in which it would be "structurally impracticable" to make a facility accessible because of the unique characteristics of the terrain, such as a building elevated on stilts in a flood or waterfront area.

New Construction

Although the new construction requirements became effective January 26, 1992, only new construction with first occupancy after January 26, 1993, is covered under the ADA. This means that only facilities that are designed after January 26, 1992, and in which occupancy occurs after January 26, 1993, are covered by the ADA's requirements for new construction.

TITLE III REMEDIES AND ENFORCEMENT

Title III of the ADA is enforced through the remedies and procedures of Title II of the Civil Rights Act of 1964. Any person discriminated against in public accommodations or commercial facilities can do one of three things under the ADA:

- Sue for damages
- File a complaint with the attorney general
- Obtain an injunction through a federal district court to order that facilities be made readily accessible, that auxiliary aids or services be provided, that policies be modified or that alternative methods be provided

The attorney general has the authority to investigate Title III violations and to conduct compliance reviews to certify that state or local building codes comply with ADA accessibility guidelines. The law does not specify how these periodic reviews will be performed, but on-site inspections are most likely. The attorney general may bring or join a civil suit against persons engaged in a pattern and practice of discrimination and may sue on behalf of others in cases that present issues of general public importance.

The ADA prescribes a maximum civil penalty of $50,000 for the first violation and a maximum of $100,000 for subsequent violations. Punitive damages are not awarded, but attorney's fees are recoverable to prevailing parties under Title III. With respect to civil penalties, all good-faith efforts will be taken into consideration.

Even if an individual with a disability chooses not to accept an accommodation, he or she may still obtain remedies. Nothing in the act requires an individual with disabilities to accept any particular accommodation made on his or her behalf. The ADA encourages informal resolution of claims, but alternative methods such as mediation or arbitration are entirely voluntary. An individual can still file suit without exhausting these informal procedures.

SITUATION ANALYSIS

Situation

Janice S. is a personnel consultant on a disability leave of absence with a five-person employment agency. She has worked there for three years, but due to a skiing accident she is now in a wheelchair.

Janice studied the ADA during her convalescence and knows that employment agencies are covered. The office building where the agency is located has no access for a wheelchair, no elevator, and doors that are too narrow for a wheelchair to enter. Even if she were able to enter the building, the office is cramped and would need rearrangement to allow her to work.

Janice has called the EEOC to find out what she can do. What will they say?

Analysis. Bad news for Janice. The agency is exempt from ADA regulation because of its size. Currently, an employer must have 25 or more people on staff, including part-timers, to fall under ADA regulation. This number will be reduced to 15 in July 1994.

With regard to accessibility, Title III of the ADA contains detailed specifications about structural changes required in office buildings, but they do not apply to existing buildings unless they would affect "the usability of or access to an area containing a primary function."

Here, remodeling the ground-floor lobby for a bank tenant would require complete downstairs "path of travel" accommodations for a wheelchair. Remodeling the third floor would entail entrance access, an elevator, wider doors on the third floor, handrails, and other accommodations.

Although employment agencies are "covered entities" under the ADA, they are not automatically covered as to access for employees.

CHAPTER SIXTEEN

ADA Accessibility Guidelines

On July 26, 1991, the Architectural and Transportation Barriers Compliance Board issued the Americans with Disabilities Act Accessibility Guidelines for Buildings and Facilities, known by the acronym ADAAG. Following is an overview of those guidelines (see also Figure 16.1).

STANDARDS FOR EXISTING BUILDINGS

Space Allowances for Wheelchairs

The minimum clear width for a single wheelchair passage is 32 inches. The minimum width for two wheelchairs to pass is 60 inches. The space required for a wheelchair to make a 180-degree turn is a clear space of 5 feet in diameter or 5 feet square to perform such activities as returning a tool to a bin or a book to a library shelf. The minimum clear floor space required to accommodate a stationary wheelchair and occupant is 30 by 48 inches. This could be considered "standing room" for performing job tasks such as operating a drill press or sorting mail. If the employee is seated in a wheelchair at a table or desk, then the free floor space underneath the work surface can be included in the above measurements.

If the clear floor space allows a forward approach to objects such as time clocks, light switches, and electrical outlets, the maximum upward reach is 48 inches; the minimum low reach is 15 inches. If the clear floor space allows a parallel approach, the maximum upward reach is 54 inches and the low reach is no less than 9 inches above the floor.

Wheelchairs need a clear opening width of 32 inches to pass through doorways. Along corridors, aisles, tunnels, or other passageways, 36 inches is needed to accommodate the chair without scraping the occupant's hands against the side walls. If a passageway has less than 60 inches clear width, then passing spaces of at least 60 by 60 inches must be located at 200-foot intervals.

Although people who use walking aids can maneuver through clear width openings of 32 inches, they need 36-inch-wide passageways and walks for comfortable gaits. Crutch tips, often extending down at a wide angle, are a hazard in narrow passageways where they might not be seen by other pedestrians. Thus, the 36-inch width provides a safety allowance both for the person with a disability and for others.

Accessible Routes

People with mobility impairments need an accessible path of travel extending from the nearest public transportation stop, adjacent parking lot, passenger drop-off point, or public sidewalk to a handicapped-accessible building entrance. This route should coincide with the route for the general public as closely as possible.

If an accessible route has changes in level greater than $\frac{1}{2}$ inch, perhaps where two buildings were connected into one, then a ramp or platform lift must be installed. If the change in level is a story or more, a conventional elevator may be necessary.

Curb Ramps

When an accessible route crosses a curb, such as at an intersection, the curb should have a ramp at least 36 inches wide. People with visual impairments can be alerted to the curb ramp's location, and to the danger of traffic, by a detectable warning built into the walking surface. Warning textures can be made in concrete ramps by scoring the surface, applying raised strips, or using a contrasting texture. Transitions from ramps to streets must be flush and free of abrupt changes.

Parking and Passenger Loading Zones

Parking spaces for people with disabilities should be located on the shortest accessible route of travel from the parking lot to an accessible entrance. These parking spaces must be at least 96 inches wide, with an adjacent access aisle at least 60 inches wide to allow enough room for a wheelchair to pass between cars. Accessible parking spaces must be designated by a sign showing the international symbol of accessibility.

Entrances

Entrances must be connected by an accessible route to public transportation stops, to accessible parking and passenger loading zones, and to public streets or sidewalks. They must also be connected by an accessible route to all accessible spaces within the building. A service entrance must not be the only accessible entrance.

Areas of Rescue Assistance

Because people with disabilities may visit or work in virtually any building, emergency management plans with specific provisions to ensure their safe evacuation play an essential role in fire safety. A 48-inch-wide exit stairway is needed to allow assisted evacuation without encroaching on the path for ambulatory persons. All accessible routes should comply with the egress requirements established by local fire codes and building authorities so that people with disabilities have an equal chance of evacuation. Emergency communication cannot depend on voice communications alone because the safety of people with hearing or speech impairments could be jeopardized. The visible signal requirement could be satisfied with something as simple as a button in the area of rescue assistance that lights to indicate that help is on the way.

Protruding Objects

Fire extinguishers, wall-hung telephones, and other objects protruding from walls and ceilings can cause injuries. Any object that is mounted between 27 and 80 inches above the floor and protrudes more than 4 inches from the wall should be recessed.

An individual who is visually impaired needs 80 inches of clear headroom in circulation areas. Water pipes, signs, fans, and other objects suspended from the ceiling should never descend below 80 inches into the path of travel. If they do, a guard rail or other detectable barrier should be installed to warn of the threat of striking one's head.

Floor Surfaces

Floor surfaces must be stable, firm, and slip resistant. If carpeting is used, it should have a firm, nonskid backing and a level texture with a pile height of no more than ½ inch. Exposed edges of area rugs must have a continuous trim and be fastened to the floor. If there are gratings in a floor surface, the spaces must be no more than ½ inch wide.

Ramps

Any part of an accessible route with a slope greater than 1 inch for each 20 feet of approach space must be considered a ramp. People who use wheelchairs have varying strengths in their arms and shoulders, so the least possible slope will suit the most people. The maximum slope of a ramp is 1:12. This means that if the vertical rise is 1 foot, the length of the ramp should be 12 feet. In an older building where space limitations prohibit the use of a 1:12 slope, a 1:8 slope can be used for a maximum rise of 3 inches.

The minimum clear width of a ramp is 36 inches. Ramps must have level landings of 60 inches clear at bottom and top. If a ramp makes a turn, a level 60-by-60-inch landing is required.

If a ramp run has a rise greater than 6 inches, it must have handrails on both sides. They should be mounted between 30 and 34 inches above the surface of the ramp and protrude from the wall 1½ inches to allow room for gripping.

Ramps and landings with drop-offs must have curbs, walls, or railings to prevent people from slipping over the side. Outdoor ramps must be designed so that water will not accumulate on walking surfaces.

Stairs

All steps within a flight of stairs should have uniform riser heights and uniform tread widths. Treads should be no less than 11 inches wide from riser to riser. Open risers are not permitted. Stairways must have handrails at both sides of all stairs. The clear space between handrails and wall should be 1½ inches.

Elevators

People with disabilities should not have to use a freight elevator unless it is recognized and used by all employees or customers as a combination passenger-freight elevator. There are several points to consider in making an elevator convenient for people with disabilities. The car should be self-leveling and flush with floor landings. The call buttons in lobbies and halls should be placed 42 inches above the floor. The floor selection buttons in the elevator car should be no less than ¾ inch in their smallest dimension and have raised letters and numerals. If braille characters are used, they should be placed immediately to the left of the button to which they relate. Buttons should be no higher than 54 inches above the floor if there is room in the elevator for a wheelchair to make a parallel approach to the control panel, or 48 inches for a forward approach. A visible and audible signal should indicate when the car is arriving at a floor. Once the automatic doors open, there should be at least a 3-second delay before they begin to close.

Doors

A revolving door or turnstile cannot be the only means of passage. An alternative accessible doorway or gate must be provided for people who use wheelchairs, crutches, or canes. Doorways must have a minimum clear opening of 32 inches with the door open 90 degrees.

The minimum space between two doors in a series is 48 inches plus the width of any door swinging into the space. Doors in series must swing either in the same direction or away from the space between the doors.

Handles, latches, and other operating devices on accessible doors must have a shape that is easy to grasp with one hand and does not require tight gripping or twisting of the wrist to operate. Hardware should be mounted no higher than 48 inches above the finished floor. If a door has a closer, the timing must be adjusted so that the door will take at least 3 seconds to move from an open position of 70 degrees to a point 3 inches from the latch. The maximum allowable force for pushing or pulling open a door is about 5 pounds.

Drinking Fountains

Fountains and coolers can be used by a person from a wheelchair if the spout is no higher than 36 inches from the floor. The spout must be located at the front of the unit and must direct the flow of water parallel to the front of the unit. The water flow must be at least 4 inches high to allow a cup or glass to be inserted. Controls must be front mounted or side mounted near the front edge. Wall-mounted units need 27 inches of knee space underneath and at least 30 by 48 inches of clear floor space to allow a forward approach from a wheelchair. Freestanding units without knee space underneath can accommodate a parallel approach if they have the same clear floor space in front.

Signage

Characters and numbers on signs should be sized according to the viewing distance from which they are to be read. The minimum height is measured using an upper case *X*. Raised characters should be at least ⅝ inch high but no higher than 2 inches. Characters must contrast with their background—either light characters on a dark background or vice versa.

Signs that are permanently affixed to identify rooms should be installed on the wall adjacent to the latch side of the door if possible. Mounting height should be 60 inches above the floor to the centerline of the sign. A person should be able to approach to within 3 inches of the sign without encountering protruding objects or standing within the swing of a door.

Accessible facilities should be identified with the international symbol of accessibility or the international symbol of access for hearing loss.

Telephones

A wall-mounted public telephone should have at least 30 by 48 inches of clear floor space to allow for either a forward or parallel approach from a wheelchair. Bases and seats must not impede the approach. The highest operable part of the telephone must be between 48 and 54 inches (depending on the method of approach) above the floor. Where possible, telephones must have pushbutton controls. The cord from the telephone to the handset must be at least 29 inches long.

If there is a bank of public telephones, such as in the lobby of an office building, then there should also be volume control equipment to accommodate people with hearing impairments. Some employers are also providing telecommunications devices. Volume controls should range from a minimum of 12 decibels to a maximum of 18 decibels above normal.

Text telephones used with pay telephones must be permanently affixed within or adjacent to the telephone enclosure. If an acoustic coupler is used, the phone cord must be long enough to allow the text telephone to be hooked up to the telephone receiver. Pay telephones designed to accommodate a portable text telephone must be equipped with a shelf and an electrical outlet.

Restrooms

Toilet Stalls   Toilet stalls generally have to be wider or deeper than conventional ones, with enough room to transfer from a wheelchair to the toilet seat. The exact dimensions depend upon whether the water closet is wall mounted or floor mounted, whether the stall door opens inward or outward, whether the partitions between stalls provide toe clearance of at least 9 inches, whether grab bars diminish the clear floor space, and whether the flush controls and toilet paper dispenser are within reach.

Water Closets   Clear floor space may be arranged to allow either a left-handed or right-handed approach. The height of the water closet from the floor to the top of the toilet seat must be between 17 and 19 inches. Seats must not be sprung to return to a lifted position. The grab bar behind the water closet must be at least 36 inches long.

Urinals Urinals can be stall type or wall hung at a maximum of 17 inches above the floor. If privacy shields are used, a clear floor space 30 by 48 inches must be provided in front of urinals to allow forward approach.

Lavatories and Mirrors Lavatories must be mounted with the rim or counter surface no higher than 34 inches above the floor and must provide a clearance of at least 29 inches above the floor to the bottom of the apron, with adequate knee and toe clearance. A clear floor space 30 by 48 inches must be provided in front of a lavatory to allow forward approach, and extend a maximum of 19 inches underneath the lavatory. Hot water and drain pipes under lavatories must be insulated or configured to protect against contact. There can be no sharp or abrasive surfaces under lavatories.

Mirrors should be mounted with the bottom edge of the reflecting surface no higher than 40 inches above the finish floor.

Storage Facilities and Operating Mechanisms

A clear floor space of at least 30 by 48 inches that allows either a forward or parallel approach must be provided at cabinets, shelves, closets, and drawers. Clothes rods or shelves must be no more than 54 inches above the floor for a side approach. Touch latches and U-shaped pulls are appropriate hardware for storage facilities. These specifications also apply to light switches, valves, blinds and drapery pulls, vending machine controls, and other operating mechanisms.

Seating

Seating at tables, counters, or work surfaces should have enough floor space and knee space to accommodate people in wheelchairs. The knee space must be at least 27 inches high, 30 inches wide, and 19 inches deep. The tops of tables and work surfaces should be from 28 to 34 inches from the floor. If possible, they should be adjustable so they can be raised or lowered to meet individual needs.

Assembly Areas

When the seating capacity in assembly areas and company auditoriums exceeds 300, wheelchair spaces must be provided in more than one location. Wheelchair spaces must adjoin an accessible route that also serves as a means of egress in case of emergency. Readily removable seats may be installed in wheelchair spaces when the spaces are not needed to accommodate wheelchair users.

Alarms

To be effective, an emergency warning system should include both audible and visual alarms. The sound levels for audible alarms should not exceed 120 decibels, and flashing visual signals should have a frequency of about one flash per second.

Signs that provide emergency information or directions should use raised characters.

Hazard Warnings

People with visual impairments need a standardized system for identifying hazardous areas in a building. Detectable warnings on walking surfaces can be made by changing the texture of the surface or contrasting it with surrounding surfaces. Raised strips, grooves, cushioned surfaces, and roughened concrete are some ways to identify a path leading to a danger area. If a pedestrian walk or aisle crosses an area frequently used by vehicular traffic such as forklift trucks, some detachable warning should be used.

Doors that lead to boiler rooms, platforms, or any areas that might be dangerous should be identifiable to the touch by a textured surface on the door handle or other operating hardware. This can be done by knurling or roughening the knob or by applying tape to the contact surface.

STANDARDS FOR NEW CONSTRUCTION AND ALTERATIONS

Newly constructed buildings and buildings that are substantially altered or remodeled must adhere to the technical specifications outlined above. For these buildings, there are also requirements governing the number of accessible entrances, parking spaces, telephones, and seats that must be provided.

Elevators

Newly constructed office buildings that have fewer than three stories or less than 3,000 square feet of space per floor need not have elevator access to the upper floor. This means that a new two-story office building will not have to have an elevator even if each story has 20,000 square feet of space, nor would a five-story facility with 2,500 square feet of space on each floor. The elevator exemption does not apply to shopping centers, shopping malls, or the professional offices of health care providers. These facilities must have elevators regardless of square footage or number of floors.

Table 16.1   Required Number of Accessible Parking Spaces

Total Parking Spaces in Lot	Required Number of Accessible Spaces
1 to 25	1
26 to 50	2
51 to 75	3
76 to 100	4
101 to 150	5
151 to 200	6
201 to 300	7

Parking

The number of accessible parking spaces should be provided in accordance with Table 16.1.

Entrances

Because entrances also serve as emergency exits, it is best that *all* entrances be accessible. In terms of the ADA's new-construction requirements, however, at least 50 percent of all public entrances must be accessible and at least one must be a ground-floor entrance. (This does not include loading or service entrances.) An accessible entrance must be provided to each tenant in a facility: for example, to individual stores in a strip shopping center. If possible, accessible entrances should be the ones used by most people visiting or working in the building.

The number of accessible entrances must be equivalent to the number of exits required by the building fire codes. This does not require an increase in the total number of entrances planned for a facility.

If direct access is provided for pedestrians from an enclosed parking garage to the building, at least one direct entrance from the garage to the building must be accessible. The same applies to tunnels and pedestrian walkways.

Assembly Areas

In places of assembly with fixed seating, accessible wheelchair locations must be provided consistent with the ratio shown in Table 16.2.

In addition, 1 percent, but not less than one, of all fixed seats must be aisle seats with no armrests, or with folding armrests, on the aisle side. Accessible seats should be identified by a sign or marker.

**Table 16.2   Required Number of Wheelchair Locations
in Assembly Areas**

Seating Capacity in Assembly Area	Number of Required Wheelchair Locations
4 to 25	1
26 to 50	2
51 to 300	4
301 to 500	6
over 500	6 plus 1 space for each 100 seats

Drinking Fountains

Where there is more than one drinking fountain or water cooler on a floor, 50 percent of them must be wheelchair accessible and located on an accessible route.

Where only one drinking fountain is provided on a floor, that drinking fountain should be accessible to people who use wheelchairs and at a standard height convenient for those who have difficulty bending or stooping. This can be accommodated by the use of a "hi-lo" fountain.

Telephones

If public telephones are provided, then a certain number of them must be wheelchair accessible, hearing-aid compatible, and equipped with a volume control (see Table 16.3).

In addition, 25 percent, but not less than one, of all other public telephones provided must be equipped with a volume control. If four or more public pay phones (both interior and exterior) are provided, at least one interior public text telephone must be provided.

Where a bank of telephones in the interior of a building consists of three

**Table 16.3   Acquired Number of Accessible and
Specially Equipped Telephones**

Number of Phones on Each Floor	Number of Accessible and Specially Equipped Phones
1 or more single units	1 per floor
1 bank*	1 per floor
2 or more banks	1 per bank

*A bank is two or more adjacent phones.

or more public pay phones, at least one telephone in each bank must be equipped with a shelf and an outlet to accommodate a portable text telephone.

Built-in Tables and Seating

If fixed or built-in seating or tables (as in student laboratory stations or library carrels) are provided in public or common use areas, at least 5 percent, but not less than one, of the seats or tables must be wheelchair accessible. An accessible route must lead to and through the accessible seating area.

CHECKLIST FOR EVALUATING THE ACCESSIBILITY OF YOUR FACILITY

Parking
- Are there spaces reserved for handicapped drivers?
- Is the space adequately marked with the international symbol of access?
- Is the accessible parking space as close as possible to an accessible building entrance (no more than 200 feet distance)?
- Is the parking space at least 8 feet wide, plus adjacent aisle space of 5 feet for a wheelchair to pass between cars?
- Is the route from the parking space to the accessible building entrance free of barriers such as curbs, steps, shrubbery, and fences?
- Is the number of spaces used by drivers who are disabled in accordance with the frequency and persistency of parking needs?

Ramps
- If a ramp is used to circumvent steps or other level changes, is it at least 36 inches wide?
- Is the slope or gradient of the ramp no more than a 1-foot rise in 12 feet?
- Are handrails on ramps between 30 and 34 inches high from the surface of the ramp?
- Do ramps have a nonslip surface?
- Do lengthy ramps have level platforms at 30-foot intervals and wherever the ramp turns for purposes of rest and safety?
- Does the ramp have level landings of 5-foot lengths at the top and bottom along the path of travel?

Entrance and Doorway
- Is there at least one primary entrance that is approached by a level or ramped walk?

- Is at least one entrance usable by individuals in wheelchairs on a floor accessible to the elevator?
- When the door is open, is there at least 32 inches of clear space for a wheelchair to pass through?
- Are the doors operable with pressure or strength that could reasonably be expected from a person with a disability?
- Is there an unobstructed level area inside and outside each doorway for at least 5 feet to allow a wheelchair to avoid the swing of the door?
- Is the threshold less than ½ inch high? Is it beveled?

Elevators
- In buildings taller than one story, are elevators available to people with disabilities?
- Does the elevator cab automatically come level with the lobby or corridor floor?
- Is the control panel installed so that the highest button is within 54 inches of the floor?
- Does the panel have raised symbols or numbers to permit persons who are visually impaired to select their floor?

Restrooms
- Do entry doors have a 32-inch clear opening?
- If there is a vestibule between two doors, is there a minimum space of 48 inches between the series of doors, not counting the width of any door swinging into the space?
- Do toilet rooms have enough turning space for people in wheelchairs?
- Is the height of the water closet between 17 and 19 inches when measured from floor to top of toilet seat?
- Do lavatories have an underneath clearance of 29 inches measured from the floor?
- Are there grab bars fastened between 33 and 36 inches from the floor? Is there a 1½-inch space between the wall and the grab bar?
- Do toilet rooms have at least one toilet stall with a 32-inch-wide opening outward? Does the stall have a minimum depth of 56 inches and minimum width of 60 inches?
- Are drain pipes and hot water pipes covered or insulated?
- Are mirrors mounted with the bottom edge no higher than 40 inches from the floor?

Drinking Fountains
- Is the spout of the fountain no higher than 36 inches from the floor?
- Are the spout and the controls near the front of the unit?
- With cantilevered units, is there knee clearance between the bottom of the fountain and the floor? Do freestanding units without clear space under them have floor space in front at least 30 by 48 inches to allow for parallel approach in a wheelchair?

Public Telephones
- If public telephones are provided, are the highest operable parts no higher than 54 inches from the floor?
- Are telephones available that are equipped for persons with hearing impairments? Are they identified as such?
- Is there clear floor space at each accessible public telephone of at least 30 by 48 inches?

Work Surfaces
- Are the tops of tables and work surfaces 28 to 34 inches from the floor? Different types of work require different surface heights for comfort and performance. Writing, for instance, requires a higher work surface than manual work.

Alarms
- Does the emergency warning system include both audible and visual alarms?

Warning Signals
- Are there walking surfaces textured to indicate approaching hazardous areas such as tops of stairs?
- Are there tactile warnings on doors to hazardous areas such as loading platforms, boiler rooms, or fire escapes?

Signage
- Is the international symbol of access used to indicate general circulation directions or identify rooms and spaces that are accessible to people with disabilities?

Source: *Employees Are Asking about Making the Workplace Accessible to Workers with Disabilities.* Washington, DC: President's Committee on Employment of People with Disabilities, 1991.

CHAPTER SEVENTEEN

Recap: Some Common Questions and Answers about the ADA

Should I tell my employer that I have a disability?

If you think you'll need an accommodation to complete the job application process or to perform essential job functions, you will have to discuss your disability with the employer. Employers are required to accommodate only those limitations they are aware of. It is the employee's responsibility to inform the employer that an accommodation is needed.

Do I have to pay for the accommodations I need?

No. The Americans with Disabilities Act (ADA) requires that the employer provide the accommodation unless it would impose an undue hardship on the business. In that case, the employee must be allowed to pay for the portion that causes the undue hardship.

Under what circumstances can an employer establish physical criteria for a job?

An employer can apply any criterion that is job related and consistent with business necessity. If lifting 50-pound boxes is essential to a particular job, an employer can require that an applicant for that position be able to

Note: Questions and responses excerpted in part from *Task Force Report on the Americans with Disabilities Act*, prepared by Littler, Mendelson, Fastiff & Tichy, 1991.

lift 50 pounds. If the person could perform the lifting with a reasonable accommodation, the employer may not deny that individual the job.

If there are two applicants for a position and one is disabled, is the employer obliged to hire that person?
No. If the nondisabled applicant is more qualified for the job in question, the employer may hire that person, as long as the determination was not based on criteria that discriminate on the basis of disability.

However, the employer may not use an applicant's ability to perform *nonessential* functions of the job as part of the selection process. If answering the phone was not an essential function of a typist's job, an employer could not choose a hearing applicant over a hearing-impaired applicant if both were equally qualified to perform the essential job functions.

Can an employer refuse to hire someone whose disability might be dangerous to others?
Yes. The standard that a person not pose a direct threat to the health or safety of others in the workplace is legitimate. The key term here is *direct*. The risk involved must be a significant one that cannot be eliminated by reasonable accommodation.

Some companies require all applicants to undergo a medical examination. Is this still permitted under the ADA?
An employer may require a medical examination only *after* an offer of employment is made and *before* the applicant starts the job. The offer of employment may be conditioned on the results of the examination.

Can I be sure that information I give an employer about my disability is confidential?
Your records are confidential. The ADA stipulates that supervisors may be informed of any restrictions on your duties or any accommodations that are necessary for you on the job. The employer also may inform first-aid or safety personnel and government officials who are investigating violations of the ADA.

Can a company test employees or applicants for drugs?
The ADA places no restrictions on drug testing of applicants or employees, as long as the tests are designed to identify illegal drugs.

Is a personnel policy that prohibits illegal use of drugs and alcohol at the company still acceptable under the ADA?
An employer may require that employees abstain from using alcohol or drugs at the workplace. The ADA is not meant to undercut the requirements established under the Drug Free Workplace Act of 1988.

If state law provides different protections for people with disabilities than those in the ADA, which law would apply?

The ADA does not invalidate or limit state laws that provide greater or equal protection to individuals with disabilities.

If the health insurance offered by my employer does not cover all of the medical expenses related to my disability, does the company have to obtain additional coverage for me?
No. The ADA only requires that an employer provide employees with disabilities equal access to whatever health insurance coverage is offered to other employees.

Can insurance companies or employers deny health insurance coverage to someone on the basis of their disability?
No. All people with disabilities must have equal access to the health insurance coverage that the employer provides to all employees. A limitation may be placed on reimbursement for a procedure or the types of drugs or procedures covered, but that limitation must apply to persons with or without disabilities.

Can insurance companies or employers continue plans that limit certain kinds of coverage based on classification or risk?
Yes. However, an insurer may not refuse to continue insuring an individual or charge a different rate for the same coverage without sound actuarial evidence or reasonable anticipated experience. Employers may continue to offer policies that exclude preexisting conditions even though such exclusions adversely affect people with disabilities. Similarly, while an insurer can deny coverage for a preexisting condition for a time, the coverage may not be denied for illnesses unrelated to the preexisting condition.

Is an overweight person covered by the ADA?
Probably not. Being overweight is simply a physical characteristic. However, if a person's obesity causes a physiological disorder, such as difficulty in breathing, that would be covered under the ADA.

Does the ADA cover people with AIDS?
Yes. Under the ADA, a person suffering from a contagious disease is considered disabled. This includes people with AIDS and those who test positive for HIV.

I think I was discriminated against because my wife is disabled. Can I file a charge with the Equal Employment Opportunity Commission?
Yes. The ADA makes it unlawful to discriminate against a person because of a relationship or association with an individual with a known disability.

Would a person who was not hired because he or she wore glasses be covered?
Yes. A person wears glasses to compensate for a visual impairment. This

physiological disorder substantially limits the major life activity of seeing, even though the disorder may be corrected through the use of glasses.

If I break my arm and am temporarily unable to perform the essential functions of my job as a machinist, am I protected by the ADA?
No. Although you do have an impairment, it does not substantially limit a major life activity if it is of limited duration and will have no long-term effect.

Is a pregnant employee protected under the ADA?
Pregnancy is one of several conditions that are excluded from ADA protection. Others include homosexuality, bisexuality, transvestism, pedophilia, voyeurism, compulsive gambling, kleptomania, and pyromania.

Does an employer have to make changes in the workstation to accommodate left-handed people?
No. Simple physical traits such as left-handedness, blue eyes, or fair skin do not constitute impairments under the ADA.

What is job restructuring?
Job restructuring refers to modifying a job so that a person with a disability can perform the central functions of the position. Barriers to performance may be removed by eliminating nonessential elements of the job, redelegating assignments, exchanging assignments with another employee, or redesigning procedures. The key to job restructuring is flexibility.

Must an employer bump another employee out of a position to accommodate a disabled person?
No. The reassignment need only be to a *vacant* position. Another employee need not be bumped to create a vacancy.

Is a collective bargaining agreement relevant in determining whether a given accommodation is reasonable?
Yes. If a collective bargaining agreement reserves certain jobs for employees with a given amount of seniority, it may be considered as a factor in determining whether it is a reasonable accommodation to assign an employee with a disability without seniority to the job.

What if I refuse to accept an accommodation that my employer offers?
The ADA provides that an employer cannot require a qualified individual with a disability to accept an accommodation that is not requested or needed. However, if a necessary reasonable accommodation is refused, the individual may be considered not qualified.

Who has responsibility for removing barriers in a shopping mall—the landlord who owns the property or the tenant who leases the store?
Both landlord and tenant have responsibilities unless a clearly defined

agreement is in place. In most cases, the landlord will have full control over common areas.

If a business has a fitness room for the staff, must it be accessible to employees with disabilities?
Yes. Under the ADA, workers with disabilities must have equal access to all benefits and privileges of employment. The duty to provide reasonable accommodation applies to all nonwork facilities—cafeterias, lounges, auditoriums, transportation, and counseling services.

If my employer holds a staff training program at a hotel that is inaccessible to some of its employees, is the company in violation of the ADA?
Yes. An employer may not do through a third party what it is prohibited from doing directly. The employer would have to provide a site that is readily accessible to employees with disabilities unless doing so would create an undue hardship.

How does the ADA recognize public health concerns?
The ADA recognizes the need to strike a balance between the right of a disabled person to participate in the mainstream of American life and the right of the public to be protected from legitimate health threats. The ADA is not intended to supplant the role of public health authorities in protecting the community.

Will businesses need to install elevators?
Businesses are not required to retrofit their facilities to install elevators unless such installation is readily achievable. Even in new buildings, elevators are not required in structures under three stories in height or with fewer than 3,000 square feet per floor unless the building is a shopping center or professional office of a health care provider.

Will restaurants be required to have braille menus?
No, not if waiters or other employees are made available to read the menu to a blind customer.

Will businesses need to rearrange furniture and display racks?
Possibly. Restaurants may need to rearrange tables, and department stores may need to adjust their layout of racks and shelves to permit wheelchair access.

If I'm injured on the job, am I protected by the ADA?
An injury and a disability are not necessarily the same thing. Whether an injured worker is protected by the ADA will depend on whether the person meets the ADA definition of a "qualified individual with a disability." The person's injury must substantially limit a major life activity. A worker who can no longer perform the essential functions of the job with or without an

accommodation must be considered for a vacant position at the same or lower grade level for which he or she is qualified.

The fact that an employee is awarded worker's compensation benefits does not automatically establish that this person is protected by the ADA because many work-related injuries are not severe enough or long-term enough to substantially limit a major life activity. The definition of a disability under most state laws differs from the ADA's. State worker's compensation laws are designed to assist workers who suffer many kinds of injuries whereas the ADA is meant to protect people from discrimination on the basis of a disability.

What if I lie about my physical condition?

An employer can fire or refuse to hire a person who knowingly provides a false answer to a lawful postoffer inquiry about his or her condition or worker's compensation history.

Some state laws release an employer from its obligation to pay worker's compensation benefits if an employee misrepresents his or her physical condition when hired and is later injured as a result.

What are my rights if I'm injured on the job?

If your injury affects your ability to perform the essential functions of the job, the employer would probably be allowed to require a medical examination on the basis of business necessity. However, the employer can require only a *job-related* medical examination, not a complete physical, as a condition of returning to work.

An employer cannot refuse to let someone with a disability return to work because the person is not fully recovered unless he or she cannot perform the essential functions of the job with or without reasonable accommodation or would pose a significant risk of substantial harm to him- or herself or others.

Can a person file a discrimination charge against an employer on more than one basis?

Yes. A visually-impaired worker can claim that she was discriminated against on the basis of both her sex and her disability. She can file a single charge alleging both forms of discrimination.

Resources

ORGANIZATIONS

ABLEDATA
8455 Colesville Road
Silver Spring, MD 20910-3319
800/346-2742 or 800/227-0216
301/588-9284
A consumer referral service that maintains a data base of more than 17,000 adaptive devices from 2,000 companies.

Accent on Information
P.O. Box 700
Bloomington, IL 61702
309/378-2961

ACTION
1100 Vermont Avenue, N.W.
Washington, DC 20525
800/424-8867

Adaptive Device Locator System
Academic Software
331 W. 2nd Street
Lexington, KY 40507
606/233-2332

Administration on Developmental Disabilities
U.S. Department of Health and Human Services
200 Independence Avenue, S.W.
Washington, DC 20201
202/245-2890
202/245-2897 (TDD)

Advanced Rehabilitation Technology Network
25825 Eshelman Avenue
Lomita, CA 90717
310/325-3058

Alliance for Technology Access
1128 Solano Avenue
Albany, CA 94706
510/528-0747

American Cancer Society
1599 Clifton Road, N.E.
Atlanta, GA 30329
800/227-2345

American Council of the Blind
1155 15th Street, N.W.
Washington, DC 20005
800/424-8666

American Federation of Labor
& Congress of Industrial
Organizations
815 16th Street, N.W.
Washington, DC 20006
202/637-5000

American Foundation for
Technology Assistance
Route 14, Box 230
Morganton, NC 28655
704/438-9697

American Foundation for the
Blind
15 W. 16th Street
New York, NY 10011
212/620-2000
212/620-2158 (TT)

American Occupational Therapy
Association
1383 Piccard Drive
Rockville, MD 20849
800/843-2682

American Paralysis Foundation
500 Morris
Springfield, NJ 07081
800/225-0292

American Parkinson's Disease
Association
60 Bay Street
Staten Island, NY 10301
800/223-2732

American Physical Therapy
Association
1111 N. Fairfax Street
Alexandria, VA 22314
703/684-2782

American Printing House for
the Blind
1839 Frankfort Avenue
Louisville, KY 40206
800/223-1839

American Society of
Handicapped Physicians
105 Morris Drive
Bastrop, LA 71220
318/281-4436

American Speech-Language-
Hearing Association
10801 Rockville Pike
Rockville, MD 20852
800/638-8255
301/897-5700

American Tinnitus Association
P.O. Box 5
Portland, OR 97207
503/248-9985

Apple Computer
Worldwide Disability Solutions
Group
20525 Mariani Avenue
Cupertino, CA 95014
408/974-7910
408/974-7911 (TDD)

Architectural and
Transportation Barriers
Compliance Board
1331 F Street, N.W.
Washington, DC 20004
800/USA-ABLE
202/272-5434
*A federal entity; has a technical
assistance hotline for
organizations that must comply
with the Americans with
Disabilities Act (ADA).*

Arthritis Foundation
1314 Spring Street, N.W.
Atlanta, GA 30309
800/283-7800

Assistive Device Center
6000 J Street
Sacramento, CA 95819
916/278-6422

**Assistive Technology
Information Network**
University Hospital
The University of Iowa
Iowa City, IA 55242
800/331-3027

**Association for Education and
Rehabilitation of the Blind
and Visually Impaired**
206 N. Washington Street
Alexandria, VA 22314
703/548-1884

**Association for Mental
Retardation**
500 E. Border
Arlington, TX 76010
817/261-6003

**Association for Retarded
Citizens**
National Employment and
Training Program
P.O. Box 6109
Arlington, TX 76005
817/640-0204
*A federally funded program
involved in training and placing
the disabled, with some 1,300
state and local chapters
nationwide.*

**Association of Persons in
Supported Employment**
5001 W. Broad Street
Richmond, VA 23230
804/282-3655

**AT&T National Special Needs
Center**
2001 Route 46
Parsippany, NJ 07054
800/233-1222 or 800/833-3232

Berkeley Planning Associates
440 Grand Avenue
Oakland, CA 94610
510/465-7884

Better Hearing Institute
P.O. Box 1840
Washington, DC 20013
800/327-9355

Braille Institute of America
741 N. Vermont Avenue
Los Angeles, CA 90029
213/663-1111

**Building Owners and Managers
Association International**
1201 New York Avenue, N.W.
Washington, DC 20005
202/408-2662
Publications include ADA
Compliance Guidebook: A
Checklist for Your Building.

**Bureau of Services for Visually
Impaired**
5535 Southwick Boulevard
Toledo, OH 43614
419/866-1669

Centers for Disease Control and Prevention
Public Health Service
U.S. Department of Health and Human Services
1600 Clifton Road, N.E.
Atlanta, GA 30333
404/639-2237

Clearinghouse on Computer Accommodations
General Services Administration
18 and F Streets, N.W.
KGDO #2022
Washington, DC 20405
202/501-4906

Clearinghouse on Disability Information
U.S. Department of Education
Switzer Building
400 Maryland Avenue, S.W.
Washington, DC 20202
202/708-5366

Commission on Civil Rights
1121 Vermont Avenue, N.W.
Washington, DC 20425
202/376-8312

Computer Electronic Accommodations Program
U.S. Department of Defense
5109 Leesburg Pike
Falls Church, VA 22041
703/756-8811

Congress of Organizations of the Physically Disabled
16630 Beverly Drive
Tinley Park, IL 60477
708/532-3566

Council for Disability Rights
208 S. LaSalle Street
Chicago, IL 60604
312/444-9484

Council of Better Business Bureaus
4200 Wilson Boulevard
Arlington, VA 22203
703/276-0100

Council of Citizens with Low Vision International
1400 N. Drake Road
Kalamazoo, MI 49006
616/381-9566

Council of State Administrators of Vocational Rehabilitation
1055 Thomas Jefferson Street, N.W.
Washington, DC 20007
202/638-4634
Call for information on state vocational rehabilitation agencies.

Cystic Fibrosis Foundation
6931 Arlington Road
Bethesda, MD 20814
800/344-4823

Deafness and Communicative Disorders Branch
U.S. Department of Education
Rehabilitation Services
330 C Street, S.W.
Washington, DC 20202
202/732-1401
202/732-1330 (TDD)

Direct Link for the Disabled
P.O. Box 1036
Solvang, CA 93464
805/688-1603

**Disabilities Rights Education
and Defense Fund**
2212 6th Street
Berkeley, CA 94710
800/466-4232
Offers free material and advice.

**Dole Foundation for
Employment of People with
Disabilities**
1819 H Street, N.W.
Washington, DC 20006
202/457-0318

**Electronic Industries
Foundation**
919 18th Street
Washington, DC 20006
202/955-5816

Employment Law Center
1663 Mission Street
San Francisco, CA 94103
415/864-8848

**Equal Employment Opportunity
Commission**
1801 L Street, N.W.
Washington, DC 20507
ADA Helpline: 1-800/669-EEOC
800/800-3302 (TDD)
202/663-4900
202/663-4264 (publications)
*For $25 the EEOC offers a
technical assistance manual and
a large resource directory.
Booklets available include* The
ADA: Your Responsibilities as an
Employer; The ADA: Questions
and Answers, *and* The ADA:
Your Rights as an Individual
with a Disability.

**Federal Communications
Commission**
Office of Public Affairs
1919 M Street, N.W.
Washington, DC 20036
202/532-7260 or 202/632-6999

Federation of the Handicapped
211 W. 14th Street
New York, NY 10011
212/727-4200
212/727-4324 (TDD)

**Foundation on Employment and
Disability**
3820 Del Amo Boulevard
Torrance, CA 90503
310/214-3430

Goodwill Industries of America
9200 Wisconsin Avenue
Bethesda, MD 20814-3896
301/530-6500
301/530-0836 (TDD)

**Handicapped Assistance Loan
Program**
Small Business Administration
409 3rd Street, S.W.
Washington, DC 20416
202/205-6570

HEALTH Resource Center
(Higher Education and the
Handicapped) Project of the
American Council on
Education
U.S. Department of Education
1 Dupont Circle, N.W.
Washington, DC 20036
800/544-3284

Huntington's Disease Society of America
140 W. 22nd Street
New York, NY 10011
800/345-4372

IAM Cares (International Association of Machinists and Aerospace Workers Handicapped Youth)
1300 Connecticut Avenue, N.W.
Washington, DC 20036
202/857-5200

IBM National Support Center for Persons with Disabilities
P.O. Box 2150
Atlanta, GA 30055
800/426-4832
IBM-funded nonprofit agency provides free information on thousands of computer hardware and software accommodation devices, most of which are not IBM products.

Independent Visually Impaired Enterprises
1155 15th Street, N.W.
Washington, DC 20005
202/467-5081

Internal Revenue Service
U.S. Department of the Treasury
1111 Constitution Avenue, N.W.
Washington, DC 20224
202/566-3292
800/829-4059 (TDD)

International Association of Business, Industry and Rehabilitation
P.O. Box 15242
Washington, DC 20003
202/543-6353

International Association of Jewish Vocational Services
101 Gary Court
Staten Island, NY 10314
718/370-0437

International Association of Laryngectomies
1599 Clifton Road, N.E.
Atlanta, GA 30329
404/320-3333

International Center for the Disabled
340 E. 24th Street
New York, NY 10010
212/679-0100

International Polio Network
5100 Oakland Avenue
St. Louis, MO 63110
314/361-0475

Institute for Rehabilitation and Disability Management
229½ Pennsylvania Avenue, S.E.
Washington, DC 20003
202/408-9320
Publishes The Disability Management Sourcebook.

Job Accommodation Network
P.O. Box 6123
809 Allen Hall
West Virginia University
Morgantown, WV 26506-6123
800/526-7234
A service of the President's Committee on Employment of People with Disabilities. The Job Accommodation Network (JAN) provides free consulting services to employers seeking to accommodate workers with disabilities. JAN also maintains a

large computer data base of companies across the country that have accommodated workers.

Job Training Partnership Act Programs
Office of Job Training Programs
Employment and Training
    Administration
U.S. Department of Labor
200 Constitution Avenue, N.W.
Washington, DC 20210
202/535-0580

Joseph P. Kennedy, Jr., Foundation
1350 New York Avenue, N.W.
Washington, DC 20005
202/393-1250

Just One Break
373 Park Avenue South
New York, NY 10016
212/725-2500

Leukemia Society of America
733 3rd Avenue
New York, NY 10017
800/955-4572

Lupus Foundation of America
4 Research Place
Rockville, MD 20850
800/558-0121

Mainstream, Inc.
3 Bethesda Metro Center
Bethesda, MD 20814
301/654-2400
A private, nonprofit organization that helps disabled individuals move into the workplace; publishes guides for employers on hiring the disabled.

Mental Health & Retardation Services
State Office Building, 5th Floor
Topeka, KS 66612
913/296-3774

Mental Health Policy Resource Center
1730 Rhode Island Avenue, N.W.
Washington, DC 20036
202/775-8826

Mental Retardation Associations of America
211 E. 300 South
Salt Lake City, UT 84111
801/328-1575

Muscular Dystrophy Association
3561 E. Sunrise Drive
Tucson, AZ 85718
800/223-6666

National Alliance for the Mentally Ill
2101 Wilson Boulevard
Arlington, VA 22201
703/524-7600

National Amputation Foundation
1245 150th Street
Whitestone, NY 11357
718/767-0596

National Association for Visually Handicapped
22 W. 21st Street
New York, NY 10010
212/889-3141

National Association of Rehabilitation Facilities
P.O. Box 17675
Washington, DC 20041
703/648-9300

National Association of the Deaf
814 Thayer Avenue
Silver Spring, MD 20910
301/587-1788

National Association of the Physically Handicapped
Bethesda Scarlet Oaks
440 Lafayette Avenue
Cincinnati, OH 45220
513/961-8040

National Braille Association
1290 University Avenue
Rochester, NY 14607
716/473-0900

National Braille Press
88 Saint Stephen Street
Boston, MA 02115
617/266-6160

National Cancer Care Foundation
1180 Avenue of the Americas
New York, NY 10036
212/221-3300

National Center for Disability Services
201 I. U. Willetts Road
Albertson, NY 11507
516/747-5355
516/746-3298 (TT)

National Center for Law and the Deaf
800 Florida Avenue, N.E.
Washington, DC 20002
202/651-5373

National Center for Learning Disabilities
99 Park Avenue
New York, NY 10016
212/687-7211

National Center for State Courts
ADA Clearinghouse and Resource Center
300 Newport Avenue
Williamsburg, VA 23185
804/253-2000

National Center on Employment of the Deaf
Rochester Institute of Technology
Department of Education
P.O. Box 9887
Rochester, NY 14623
716/475-6205
716/475-6500 (TDD)

National Council on Disability
800 Independence Avenue, S.W.
Washington, DC 20591
202/267-3846

National Council on Independent Living
Troy Atrium
4th Street and Broadway
Troy, NY 12180
518/274-1979
518/274-0701 (TT)

National Depressive and Manic Depressive Association
730 N. Franklin Street
Chicago, IL 60610
312/642-0049

**National Down Syndrome
  Congress**
1800 Dempster Street
Park Ridge, IL 60068
800/232-6372

**National Down Syndrome
  Society**
666 Broadway
New York, NY 10012
800/221-4602

National Easter Seal Society
70 E. Lake Street
Chicago, IL 60601
312/726-6200
312/726-4258 (TDD)

National Federation of the Blind
Job Opportunities for the Blind
1800 Johnson Street
Baltimore, MD 21230
800/638-7518
410/659-9314

National Health Council
1730 M Street, N.W.
Washington, DC 20036
202/785-3910

National Industries for the Blind
524 Hamburg Turnpike
Wayne, NJ 07474
201/595-9200

**National Industries for the
  Severely Handicapped**
2235 Cedar Lane
Vienna, VA 22182
703/560-6800

**National Information Center on
  Deafness**
Gallaudet University
800 Florida Avenue, N.E.
Washington, DC 20002
202/651-5051
202/651-5052 (TDD)

National Information System
Center for Developmental
  Disabilities
University of South Carolina
Benson Building, 1st Floor
Columbia, SC 29208
803/777-4435

National Institute for the Deaf
Rochester Institute of
  Technology
One Lamb Memorial Drive
P.O. Box 9887
Rochester, NY 14623
716/475-6824

**National Institute on Disability
  and Rehabilitation Research**
400 Maryland Avenue, S.W.
Washington, DC 20202-2572
202/732-5801
202/732-5316 (TDD)
*Operates 10 regional technical
assistance centers (see below).
Your toll-free call to 800/949-
4232 will ring through to the
facility serving your area.*

National Kidney Foundation
30 E. 33rd Street
New York, NY 10016
800/622-9010

National Leadership Coalition on AIDS
1730 M Street, N.W.
Washington, DC 20036
202/429-0930

National Library Services for the Blind and Physically Handicapped
The Library of Congress
1291 Taylor Street, N.W.
Washington, DC 20542
202/707-5100
202/707-0744 (TDD)

National Mental Health Association
1021 Prince Street
Alexandria, VA 22314
703/684-7722

National Multiple Sclerosis Society
205 E. 42nd Street
New York, NY 10017
800/624-8326

National Network of Learning Disabled Adults
808 N. 82nd Street
Scottsdale, AZ 85257
602/941-5112

National Organization on Disability
910 16th Street, N.W.
Washington, DC 20006
202/293-5960
202/293-5968 (TDD)
Operates an information clearinghouse.

National Parkinson Foundation
1501 NW 9th Avenue
Miami, FL 33136
800/327-4545

National Rehabilitation Association
633 S. Washington Street
Alexandria, VA 22314
703/836-0750
703/836-0852 (TDD)

National Rehabilitation Information Center
8455 Colesville Road
Silver Spring, MD 20910-3319
301/588-9284

National Scoliosis Foundation
72 Mt. Auburn Street
Watertown, MA 02172
617/926-0397

National Spinal Cord Injury Association
600 W. Cummings Park
Woburn, MA 01801
800/962-9629

National Stroke Association
300 E. Hampden Avenue
Englewood, CO 80110
800/367-1990

National Stuttering Project
4601 Irving Street
San Francisco, CA 94122
415/566-5324

National Technical Information Service
U.S. Department of Commerce
5285 Port Royal Road
Springfield, VA 22161
703/487-4650

Publications include Guide for Administering Employment Examinations to Handicapped Individuals, *and* Testing the Handicapped for Employment Purposes: Adaptations for Persons with Motor Handicaps.

National Tuberous Sclerosis Association
8000 Corporate Drive
Landover, MD 20785
800/225-6872

Office of Federal Contract Compliance Programs
U.S. Department of Labor
200 Constitution Avenue, N.W.
Washington, DC 20210
202/523-9501

Orton Dyslexia Society
8600 LaSalle Road
Baltimore, MD 21204
800/222-3123

Parkinson's Disease Foundation
640 W. 168th Street
New York, NY 10032
800/457-6676

People First International
P.O. Box 12642
Salem, OR 97309
503/588-5288

Polio Society
4200 Wisconsin Avenue, N.W.
P.O. Box 106273
Washington, DC 20016
301/897-8180

President's Committee on Employment of People with Disabilities
1331 F Street, N.W.
Washington, DC 20004-1107
202/376-6200
202/376-6205 (TDD)
Provides information, referral, and technical assistance to employers and employees with disabilities. Extensive list of free publications.

President's Committee on Mental Retardation
330 Independence Avenue, S.W.
Washington, DC 20201-0001
202/619-0634

Professional Rehabilitation Sector
P.O. Box 697
Brookline, MA 02146
617/566-4432

Project Access
303 E. Wacker Drive
Chicago, IL 60601
312/565-0815
Maintains the Computer Information Center, a comprehensive data base of ADA information from a variety of sources. An annual fee of $100 allows unlimited access to the data base.

Recording for the Blind
20 Roszel Road
Princeton, NJ 08540
609/452-0606

Rehabilitation Services Administration
U.S. Department of Education
Switzer Building
330 C Street, S.W.
Washington, DC 20202
202/732-1282

Research and Training Center for Accessible Housing
P.O. Box 8613
North Carolina University
Raleigh, NC 27695-8613
919/515-3082

Self-Help for Hard of Hearing People
7800 Wisconsin Avenue
Bethesda, MD 20814
301/657-2248

Senate Subcommittee on Disability Policy
113 Hart Senate Office Building
Washington, DC 20510
202/224-6265
202/224-3457 (TDD)

Sensory Aids Foundation
399 Sherman Avenue
Palo Alto, CA 94306
415/329-0430

Short Stature Foundation
17200 Jamboree Road #J
Irvine, CA 92714
800/243-9273

Sjogren's Syndrome Foundation
382 Main Street
Port Washington, NY 11050
516/767-2866

Small Business Administration
409 3rd Street, S.W.
Washington, DC 20416
202/205-6530

Small Business Legislative Council
1156 15th Street, N.W.
Washington, DC 20005
202/639-8500

Society for the Advancement of Travel for the Handicapped
347 5th Avenue
New York, NY 10016
212/447-7284

Spina Bifida Association of America
1700 Rockville Pike
Rockville, MD 20852
800/621-3141

Stroke Clubs International
805 12th Street
Galveston, TX 77550
409/762-1022

Telecommunications for the Deaf
8719 Colesville Road
Silver Spring, MD 20910
301/589-3786

Tourette Syndrome Association
42-40 Bell Boulevard
Bayside, NY 11361
800/237-0717

Travel Industry and Disabled Exchange
5435 Donna Avenue
Tarzanna, CA 91356
818/343-6339

United Cerebral Palsy Association
1522 K Street, N.W.
Washington, DC 20005
800/872-5827

U.S. Chamber of Commerce
1615 H Street, N.W.
Washington, DC 20062-2000
800/638-6582
Publications include What
Business Must Know about the
ADA.

U.S. Department of Justice
Civil Rights Division
ADA Information Line
P.O. Box 66118
Washington, DC 20035
202/514-0301
To get a copy of the Americans
with Disabilities Act, contact the
Coordination & Review Section.

U.S. Department of
Transportation
400 7th Street, S.W.
Washington, DC 20590
202/366-9305

Veterans Employment and
Training Service
U.S. Department of Labor
500 C Street, N.W.
Washington, DC 20001
202/727-3342

Wage and Hour Division
Employment
  Standards Administration
U.S. Department of Labor
200 Constitution Avenue, N.W.
Washington, DC 20210
202/523-8727
Administers regulation governing
the employment of people with
disabilities in sheltered
workshops and the disabled
workers industries.

Western Law Center for the
Handicapped
1441 W. Olympic Boulevard
Los Angeles, CA 90015
213/736-1031

World Institute on Disability
510 16th Street
Oakland, CA 94612
415/763-4100

World Rehabilitation Fund
386 Park Avenue South
New York, NY 10016
212/679-2934

National Institute on Disability and Rehabilitation Research's Regional Disability and Business Technical Assistance Centers

Region 1: New England
(CT, ME, MA, NH, RI, VT)
University of South Maine
Institute of Public Affairs
145 Newbury Street
Portland, ME 04101
207/874-6535

Region 2: Northeast
(NJ, NY, PR, VI)
United Cerebral Palsy
  Association
354 S. Broad Street
Trenton, NJ 08608
609/392-4004
609/392-7044 (TDD)

Region 3: Mid-Atlantic
(DE, DC, MD, PA, VA, WV)
Independence Center of
    Northern Virginia
2111 Wilson Boulevard
Arlington, VA 22201
703/525-3268

Region 4: Southeast
(AL, FL, GA, KY, MS, NC, SC, TN)
United Cerebral Palsy
    Association
1776 Peachtree Street
Atlanta, GA 30309
404/888-0022
404/888-9007 (TDD)

Region 5: Great Lakes
(IL, IN, MI, MN, OH, WI)
University of Illinois at Chicago
1640 W. Roosevelt Road
Chicago, IL 60608
312/413-1407
312/413-0453 (TDD)

Region 6: Southwest
(AR, LA, NM, OK, TX)
Institute for Rehabilitation and
    Research
2323 S. Shepherd Boulevard
Houston, TX 77019
713/520-0232
713/520-5136 (TDD)

Region 7: Great Plains
(IA, KS, NE, MO)
University of Missouri at
    Columbia
4816 Santana Drive
Columbia, MO 65203
314/882-3600

Region 8: Rocky Mountain
(CO, MT, ND, SD, UT, WY)
Meeting the Challenge, Inc.
3630 Sinton Road
Colorado Springs, CO 80907
719/444-0252

Region 9: Pacific
(AZ, CA, HI, NV, Pacific Basin)
Berkeley Planning Associates
440 Grand Avenue
Oakland, CA 94610
510/465-7884
800/949-4232 (TDD)

Region 10: Northwest
(AK, ID, OR, WA)
Governor's Committee on
    Disability Issues and
    Employment
P.O. Box 9046
Olympia, WA 98507
206/438-3168
206/438-3167 (TDD)
800/HELP-ADA

PUBLICATIONS

Allen, Jeffrey G., ed. *The Employee Termination Handbook.* New York: John
    Wiley & Sons, 1986.
Bakaly, Charles G., Jr. *The Modern Law of Employment Relationships.* Engle-
    wood Cliffs, NJ: Prentice-Hall, 1989, with 1991 supplement ($85).
Fasman, Zachary. *What Business Must Know About the ADA: 1992 Compli-
    ance Guide.* Washington, DC: U.S. Chamber of Commerce, 1992 ($33).
    To order, call 908/638-6582.
Frierson, James G. *Employer's Guide to the Americans with Disabilities Act.*
    Washington, DC: Bureau of National Affairs, 1992 ($45).

Hogan, Patricia, ed. *Implementing the Employment Provisions of the Americans with Disabilities Act.* New York: Faulkner & Gray, 1991 ($87). To order, call 800/535-8403.

Johnson, Mary, ed. *People with Disabilities Explain It for You.* Louisville, Ky.: Avocado Press, 1992 ($15.95). To order, call 800/338-5412.

Job Analysis under the Americans with Disabilities Act. Rosemont, Ill.: London House, 1991 (Free). To order, call 800/221-8378.

Krementz, Jill. *How It Feels to Live with a Physical Disability.* New York: Simon & Schuster, 1992 ($18). To order, call 800/338-5412.

Lawson, Joseph W.R. *The Manager's Guide to the Americans with Disabilities Act.* Chicago: Dartnell, 1991 ($129).

LOMA (previously Life Office Management Association). *The Human Resources Manager's Guide to ADA Compliance.* Atlanta: LOMA, 1992 ($90).

————. *A Manager's Guide to the ADA: A Practical Approach.* Atlanta: LOMA, 1992 ($10).

————. *ADA: The Simple Facts.* Atlanta: LOMA, 1992 ($3). To order LOMA publications, call 404/984-3780.

Lotito, Michael, et al. *Making the ADA Work for You,* 2d ed: Northridge, Calif.: Milt Wright & Associates, 1992 ($39.50).

Meeting the Needs of Employees with Disabilities. Lexington, Mass.: Resources for Rehabilitation, 1991 ($42.95). To order, call 617/862-6455.

Morrisey, Patricia. *Human Resource Executive's Survival Guide to the Americans with Disabilities Act.* Horsham, Pa.: LRP Publications, 1992 ($135).

Perritt, Henry H., Jr. *Americans with Disabilities Act Handbook,* 2d ed. New York: John Wiley & Sons, 1991.

Personnel Selection under the Americans with Disabilities Act. Rosemont, Ill.: London House, 1992 (Free). To order, call 800/221-8378.

Pimentel, Richard, et al. *What Managers and Supervisors Need to Know about the ADA.* Northridge, Calif.: Milt Wright & Associates, 1992 ($18.50).

The New Supervisor's EEO Handbook. New York: Executive Enterprises, 1992 ($9.95). To order, call 800/332-1105.

Telecommunications Devices for the Deaf: A Guide to Selection, Ordering and Installation. Washington, DC: U.S. Architectural and Transportation Barriers Compliance Board. To order, call 202/272-5434.

Index

If you're not looking here, you're hardly looking.

There are lots of publications you can turn to when you're looking for a job. But in today's tough job market, you need the National Business Employment Weekly. It not only lists hundreds of high-paying jobs available now at major corporations all across the country, it also gives you valuable strategies and advice to help you land one of those jobs. NBEW is a Wall Street Journal publication. It's the leading national job-search and career guidance publication and has been for over ten years. Pick it up at your newsstand today. Or get the next 12 issues delivered first class for just $52 by calling toll-free...

800-367-9600

National Business Employment Weekly

If you're not looking here, you're hardly looking.